DESIGN READINESS FOR LANDSCAPE ARCHITECTS

Demands on landscape architecture students' time are many and varied – when is there a chance just to sketch, and is it worth dedicating your time to the pursuit of drawing? This book shows how in short bursts you can build up your design skills using quick, relaxed sketches, which form the basis for full projects and studio work.

This book will provide you with your own image library – sources of inspiration, guidance, and short-cuts to future designs. A variety of paths leading to design discovery, based upon experimental sketching methods, are discussed, demonstrated, and then put into action with valuable exercises. These exercises focus your sketching, giving hints and tips on what to look for, how to capture the essence of the object or location, and how to become a natural in the art of speedy visual communication. Real-life examples of the author's built-works as a landscape architect show how professionals use these techniques in their own design creations.

Design Readiness for Landscape Architects presents enjoyable and thought-stirring essays and drawing-based exercises to help students grow more facile and agile in their service as architects of the land, whether using tablets, paints, or pens and pencils.

Les H. Smith is a licensed landscape architect and served as a faculty member in the Department of Landscape Architecture at Ball State University for 35 years (1982–2017). His educational background includes fine arts, performance arts, natural and social sciences, and landscape architecture. He maintains an active professional practice with a specialty in equestrian facility planning and design. Les has been recognized for his energetic and enthusiastic teaching methods. As the instructor of design-build courses, Les guides students through the design, engineering, and construction of community service projects. As a designer and teacher, he employs a distinctive design process, utilizing experimental drawing techniques to discover innovative design results.

DESIGN READINESS FOR LANDSCAPE ARCHITECTS

Drawing Exercises that Generate Ideas

LES H. SMITH

LONDON AND NEW YORK

First published 2017
by Routledge
2 Park Square, Milton Park, Abingdon, Oxon OX14 4RN

and by Routledge
711 Third Avenue, New York, NY 10017

Routledge is an imprint of the Taylor & Francis Group, an informa business

© 2017 Les H. Smith

The right of Les H. Smith to be identified as author of this work has been asserted by him in accordance with sections 77 and 78 of the Copyright, Designs and Patents Act 1988.

All rights reserved. No part of this book may be reprinted or reproduced or utilized in any form or by any electronic, mechanical, or other means, now known or hereafter invented, including photocopying and recording, or in any information storage or retrieval system, without permission in writing from the publishers.

Trademark notice: Product or corporate names may be trademarks or registered trademarks, and are used only for identification and explanation without intent to infringe.

British Library Cataloguing in Publication Data
A catalogue record for this book is available from the British Library

Library of Congress Cataloging in Publication Data
Names: Smith, Les H. (Professor of landscape architecture)
Title: Design readiness for landscape architects : drawing exercises that generate ideas / Les H. Smith.
Description: Abingdon, Oxon : Routledge, 2017. | Includes bibliographical references and index.
Identifiers: LCCN 2016043503| ISBN 9781138796157
(hardback : alk. paper) |
ISBN 9781138796164 (pbk. : alk. paper) | ISBN 9781315681986 (ebook)
Subjects: LCSH: Landscape architects—Training of. | Landscape architecture—Study and teaching. | Landscape drawing—Technique. | Drawing—Technique.
Classification: LCC SB469.6 .S65 2017 | DDC 712.092—dc23
LC record available at https://lccn.loc.gov/2016043503

ISBN: 978-1-138-79615-7 (hbk)
ISBN: 978-1-138-79616-4 (pbk)
ISBN: 978-1-315-68198-6 (ebk)

Typeset in Univers
by Keystroke, Neville Lodge, Tettenhall, Wolverhampton

CONTENTS

	Notes on the author	vii
	Preface	xi
	Acknowledgments	xiii
	Introduction	1
1	Preparing for design discovery: stretching before the run	10
2	Forms responding to systems	34
3	Field sketching to translation: the algebra and geometry of designers	59
4	Inner precedents: design ideas drawn from vigilant observation	85
5	Discovering the artistries and crafts: building design language	115
6	Ideas feed the build	132
7	Conclusion	153
	Index	158

NOTES ON THE AUTHOR

Les H. Smith was educated in the liberal arts and fine arts, then operated his own practice in landscape design-build for many of his early years. Advancing professionally, he fulfilled graduate education in Landscape Architecture, achieved licensure as a landscape architect, and soon after was awarded his Ball State University teaching position. Les has been teaching, and has been a licensed landscape architect, for 35 years – a faculty member of Ball State University's College of Architecture and Planning (CAP), Department of Landscape Architecture (LA), since 1982.

Les currently serves as a member and rotating chair on the Indiana State Board of Professional Licensing for Architects and Landscape Architects. He has served in this capacity since 2008.

A lifelong learner and enthusiastic professional, Les administers and maintains a small yet active professional practice in landscape architectural site design. He offers an expertise and specialty in planning and designing equestrian facilities. Les has designed numerous equestrian venues throughout the USA; most notably, he assisted in the design for the (Atlanta) Olympic cross-country course and equestrian venue facilities in 1996.

VIII   NOTES ON THE AUTHOR

Les is often recognized for his dedication as a mentor to his LA students and alumni. His commitment to teaching and practice is characterized by his day-to-day accessibility, his carefully delivered and detailed classes, project and field study tour preparations, and enthusiasm for teaching and providing experiential learning (immersive/entrepreneurial learning). Les places great emphasis on preparing students for a rewarding career in professional practice.

As the developer of and director for the LA Department's design-build program, Les integrates students into the design implementation aspects of the profession by helping them design, engineer, and construct community service projects (on campus and off campus). He finds the LA design-build program very rewarding as he guides students through the rigors of turning "designs on paper" into built works in the landscape – contributing needed, valued, and professional-level improvements to Muncie and its surrounding community.

As a designer–practitioner–teacher, Les is noted for encouraging his students by example – employing his exploratory design techniques. He champions the inclusion of experimental drawing methods to visualize and design landscape architectural projects. The innovative drawing methods endeavor to bond scientific and artful thinking. The experimental techniques generate unique designs, resulting in inventive built-works. He promotes the use of metaphor and figurative expressions to guide diagrammatic and design-drawing techniques that work to enrich design discoveries. Les demonstrates the connection between unique design ideas and their ability to enhance the functional needs and outcomes in real-project works, carefully serving the end users – both communities and individuals.

Les also co-directs an interdisciplinary semester-long study-travel program, offered every three years. This program takes architecture, landscape architecture, and urban planning students on an intense study-abroad program, touring through 30 countries, including over 60 cities and sites, during a four-month design-education journey.

PREFACE

Design education programs are noted for their ability to transform students' thinking and learning patterns, from "tell me how to do this," to "stand clear while I discover." *Design Readiness for Landscape Architects: Drawing Exercises that Generate Ideas* has been shaped to assist in this ongoing cause – to help designers become better designers by nurturing and boosting their inventive and innovative capabilities.

The book presents an excursion, promising students, and seasoned design professionals, ways to discovery – design discovery. It lays out a variety of maps to guide the tour, fashioning methods aimed to help designers enjoy *practicing* design. Athletes practice and train by performing calisthenics and other workouts. Designers exercise and build their design skills by sketching and drawing regularly.

Utilizing experimental drawing techniques as a means of practicing design to discover design ideas emerged from the author's own educational experiences, and throughout his career in professional practice and his design communication and design studio teaching opportunities (in the academy, as well as abroad). Many of the techniques demonstrated herein are the result of the author and his

XII   PREFACE

students working collaboratively to extend field sketching beyond its record-keeping emphasis, using drawing to reach for and capture fresh design principles and realize new design ideas.

The book has been prepared to serve a number of design education and professional development needs. In its entirety it is well suited to support a semester-long design studio class intent on helping students become freer in their design thinking and ideation processes. The book's instructions, exercises, and demonstrated techniques will serve to enrich and enliven all levels of design studio courses, from foundation to upper levels. It works equally well as an independent study guide, and can accompany design students on extended field studies (in organized or independent tours). It can also serve professionals who desire a private drawing coach while out on a coffee break or during other "me time." The instructions provide a series of self-scheduled sketching revivals – book and sketchbook in hand – out-of-office.

Students and professionals in landscape architecture are uniquely privileged to discover inspiration for their design work through many diverse avenues, venues, and experiences. Sketching and drawing continue to be clever, quick, and sustainable means of capturing and evaluating design thoughts. Visibly thinking – with pencil, pen, and sketchbook – keeps the designer fresh and equipped to conceive original and surprising design ideas. *Design Readiness for Landscape Architects* presents enjoyable and thought-stirring drawing-based exercises to help students and professionals grow more facile and agile in their design service as architects of the land.

ACKNOWLEDGMENTS

During the course of each day, true thanks must go first to the One Who unconditionally gives wholeness, as a result of the accomplished works of His perfect son. Believing is the true and vital energy source that fuels fruitful lives and productive works in service to others. To you who faithfully believe with me and back up my work, thank you, thank you, thank you.

Thanking everyone who has supported, helped, and encouraged the development and production of this book would result in another book. You each know who you are – colleagues, mentors, ministers, counselors, students, alumni, and fellow professionals. Be certain of your contributions to the author and this work. You have been and will continue to be rewarded for your assistance in making this text and its lessons available to those who choose to partake and enjoy.

Very special thanks must be extended to Adam Regn Arvidson, FASLA, PLA. Adam provided countless hours of thought, discussions, suggestions, and writing instructions throughout the project. His expertise, confirmed by his award-winning books and professional writing, along with his daily involvement in and passion

XIV   ACKNOWLEDGMENTS

for design, provided great encouragement and keen direction that are profitably woven throughout this work.

My kind and caring editor, Sadé Lee, should be knighted and given the title: *Gracious Shepherd and Book Saver*. Without Sadé's fathomless patience, bright encouragement, and "can do" cheers, this project could have become a shelf dweller, a gatherer of dust.

The dearest *thank you* is saved for last, because the giver is my best friend, partner in life – my wife, Marla. As all authors know, a book project takes on a life – its own life. It soon becomes retitled: "da book." Such an initiative can consume the author. But in this case, while sacrificing a substantial share of "us time," Marla helped both of us sustain necessary balance. She hourly and daily supported the husband, the author, and the project – each and every extended step of the way. In different ways, Marla worked just as much as I did on "da book." Her serenity, hope, and grace reside in the book and partnered with its purpose.

INTRODUCTION

REFRESHING THE ART AND SCIENCE PARTNERSHIP IN DESIGN: DRAWING AND BALANCE

Parc Güell by Antoni Gaudí in Barcelona, Spain.

Landscape architects thrive by making designs. They are tuned to heed calls. They spring to action, generating useful, original, inspiring, and fulfilling places and spaces. They are service-focused. They love to deliver good design. Design ideas come alive in drawings.

2   INTRODUCTION

Students, educators, and practitioners of landscape architecture appreciate and own their responsibilities. They enjoy working diligently. It is exhilarating to dig in and bring to light new design methodologies that respond to pressing environmental, social, cultural, economic, and ethical concerns – concerns that seem formidable. In the arena of design, pleas to solve many woes are unsettled and loud. Complex, entangled, and time-sensitive needs for healthy lands and vibrant places are eagerly nurtured by the profession. Thoughts, hands, fingers join pencils and pens, landing on sketchbook pages, striking and plotting possibilities.

Landscape architecture pledges good design while pulled into a crowd, the press of urgency. The pressures are understood and

Jardin du Luxembourg in Paris, France.

INTRODUCTION 3

careful responses generated. Urgency can be formidable. For the designer, the press of urgency is handled with poise. Conscious efforts are required, stepping back and away, retreating from the tug and tow of urgency, remaining balanced. Balance guards, restricting the rush from overtaking landscape architecture's legacy of wise and thoughtful design. Urgency can incline, even train, the profession to bring problems under control by employing expeditious, hasty, and technical design fixes. Control does not equal resolution. Control, as a motivator, does not yield good design. Quelling a rushing crowd is a delicate, sympathetic, and artful process. The practice of drawing is a settling agent. Drawing is a likeable friend and counselor, effective in sustaining balance in the search for design ideas freed from pressure.

Good and complete design requires incubation amid calm, quiet, and fresh surrounds, with peace guiding the urgency. Problem-solving and design processes need simple moments – moments of respite and harbor, beauty-rest. A pencil-hike around a sketchbook or pen floating over a napkin is refuge, a welcome sanctuary for design and designer.

Landscape architecture sustains its unique and distinctive position among the design professions. It holds fast to the enduring, well-tested, true, and faithful marriage and partnership – art and science. This union persists, molding the proficiency of land architects to solve critical design and planning problems in forms that flow naturally from drawing to place – fresh, balanced, well rested – energize landscapes.

The durable phrase "landscape architecture involves the art and science of . . ." (Newton 1971: xxix) perseveres in most definitions of the profession and practice of landscape architecture. Teaming art with science motivates discovery in design. Art and science together guide the application of discipline-relevant knowledge, fusing beauty with accountability to vital facts. United and devoted, one in the other, they formulate aesthetic and sound design performance.

Art and science are inextricably nested in good design, like a nuclear family. This charged and valiant household is the vibrant force of design, yielding consistent, lasting, insightful, and serviceable landscape design outcomes. Art and science co-author designs that are packaged in discovery, delight, and surprise (Vitruvius 1960).

Fortress wall and gate in Avignon, France.

INTRODUCTION   5

In the realm of design, art and science cooperate. When the partners are sympathetically balanced, designs prosper. Hurry-up design work can become habitual, steering a design effort towards the fix rather than holistic design outcomes. This strains the art–science affiliation. Rushing to resolve disrupts equilibrium, disabling optimum teamwork. Pressed by urgency, the science-member has inadvertently taken rein in many design initiatives – dominating and diminishing the art.

Arthur's Seat in Edinburgh, Scotland.

6   INTRODUCTION

Template-formed techniques, pre-programmed techno ogies and modeling, time-saving kit-of-parts, and trend-mirroring ooks can sneak in to drive design outcomes. These approaches unplug the design process from experimentation and innovation. The knit of art in the science, balanced and in agreement, has long clothed projects in lasting beauty. The teamwork fuels rich expression and meaning, shapes innovative resolution, and stages enduring vitality – fresh to the core (de Sausmarez 1964). The competence nurtured by infusing design with the spirit and gift of art (Henri 1923) is essential to sustain and drive forward best practices. Expressive design is fostered as art and science contribute equally – balanced and integrated.

Landscape architectural education and practice promote comprehensive, good design when the vital marriage between art and science is nurtured. Activating design education with regular and frequent analytical field sketching and experimental drawing techniques brilliantly energizes the partnership. Drawing imparts fitness to the art–science enterprise – actuating the sketchbook as art mentor and design stimulator.

DESIGN-DETECTIVE
Drawing spaces and structures in the landscape (designed and natural environments) produces much more than a static record. Field sketching and other drawing exercises build a storehouse of valuable substance for the designer's original design work. The process of drawing presents behind-the-scenes factors to the designer. Systems that form the place are observed and sensed. Spatial geometries are registered, even felt. The act of drawing appropriates and stores an array of design-relevant experiences and fertile thoughts. When a drawing grasps the soul or the "good"-ness of a particular place, one's mental design bank or design library is enlarged.

Drawing pursues design. In the process of drawing the designer becomes design-detective. Drawing gathers concepts, idea-rich possibilities, emergent principles, even criteria, all compiled for retrieval and future use. Drawing commits the designer to practice designing, to log, edit, assess, explore, and discover. Drawing enriches a designer's training and professional practice. Drawing is design experimentation, expanding the scope of visual and spatial languages employed to shape useful, expressive, and novel landscapes. Drawing stretches and reaches, generating new tools, ideas, to sculpt unique and original designs. Drawing extends the efficacy of design solutions to the benefit of those served by the profession (Hall 1976).

Tour Eiffel in Paris, France.

Garden and pool at the Alhambra in Granada, Spain.

DESIGN READINESS

To design fluidly requires preparation – exercise and practice. Experimental and exploratory drawing cultivates design readiness, preparing designers and design teams with helpful resources for design, design capital, and reserves. Practicing design stirs up ideas – ideas eager to craft inventive and inspiring landscapes. Thoughtful and spirited drawing experimentation formulates a personal, original design language. A vivid and agile visual vocabulary – an imaginative lexicon of spatial configurations and design possibilities – delivers a fruitful and energetic design process for landscape architects.

Design Readiness presents design-practice moments – moments that fuse drawing with design-thinking. The essays opening each chapter rouse design-thinking, forming an invitation to draw – to exercise, to practice as the chapters close. The drawing exercises are purposefully insulated from current project work or assignments. Framed with dialog and instruction, *Design Readiness* delivers students and professionals a variety of paths for self-learning – means to generate original design ideas. These exercises can be undertaken in private or in group settings. They are simple and free exercises As they are regularly and faithfully employed they foster success, detached from any judgment or evaluation. This array of quick and effective design drawing exercises will generate remarkable design ideas for future application.

Guard Station at the Palais Princier in Monaco.

Design Readiness is a tutorial, a user-friendly tag-along mate. It outlines mini-workshops, achievable in short sessions. Strap it to the sketchbook; carry it along with pen and pencil in pocket, ready for a brief hideaway, a moment of "me time." *Design Readiness* guides the user, encouraging the integration of field sketching with other forms of design drawing efforts. While building a personal vocabulary for design, the sequence of exercises also expands capabilities in assessing and analyzing the design of existing and proposed spaces and places. The learning sequences provided in *Design Readiness* have been generated by the author, concluding with examples of built works that benefited from these experimental design drawing techniques.

Statuary of crane symbolizing longevity in Beijing, China.

Design Readiness is an invitation to utilize drawing as a trusted partner on the path of design discovery. It is an invitation to utilize drawing as a form of learning – recreational learning. It is an invitation to make use of drawing to relax and stretch, and to work out a bit. It is an invitation to take well-deserved moments to think and draw, anticipating lively and fresh design ideas to follow.

REFERENCES

de Sausmarez, M. *Basic Design: The Dynamics of Visual Form*. New York: Van Nostrand Reinhold Co., 1964.

Hall, E. T. *Beyond Culture*. New York: Anchor Press, 1976.

Henri, R. *The Art Spirit*. Boulder, CO: Westview Press, 1923.

Newton, N. T. *Design on the Land: The Development of Landscape Architecture*. Cambridge, MA: Harvard University Press, 1971.

Vitruvius. *The Ten Books on Architecture*. Trans. Morris Hicky Morgan. Mineola, NY: Dover Publications, 1960 (first published 1914).

PREPARING FOR DESIGN DISCOVERY: STRETCHING BEFORE THE RUN

1

Synopsis: This chapter and outlined exercises encourage the student to value drawing for its complete benefits – generating ideas applicable in future design work. Drawing for the purpose of discovering ideas does require time and effort expended in experimental drawing and diagramming. The process builds up one's internal storehouse of design possibilities for future project work. The examples and exercises provided instruct how to practice design drawing, initially free of real-site or real-project constraints and variables.

Primary learning outcomes:
From knowledge acquired in this chapter, including practicing the exercises, students:

- Will understand and be conversant with a number of mental processes and

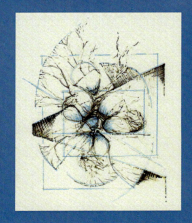

Experimental drawing expressing a synthesis of natural and built forms.

theories related to learning, emphasizing the realm of inventive visual thinking.
- Will be able to generate for themselves sketchbook-based design experiments.
- Will be able to demonstrate increased agility when using drawing and diagramming to investigate design themes (such as morphology of forms, force-influenced patterns, and interactive geometries).
- Will assemble a personal form and space idea bank, populated with self-generated design possibilities, unrestrained by pre-judgment.

Relevance to landscape architectural students and professionals: In order to generate and achieve inventive, timely, and effective design outcomes for clients and real-project work, designers cultivate and sustain agile visual-thinking capacities. Cultivating this unified set of skills (designer fitness) requires exercises and workouts, similar to athletics training.

TRACKING DESIGN DISCOVERY

Students and practitioners of landscape architectural design have access to oceans of genuine advice. Design education is flush with recommendations and teaching tools meant to help students perform more imaginatively – to be designers. Programs and manuals provide helpful suggestions on how to be more inventive and innovative when called to design. It is equally valuable and fundamental that design education provides instruction outlining the necessary preparations that fuel imagination, inventiveness, and innovation in designers. Runners stretch before the run.

The world of design education has inducted the term *creative* as the title of performance qualifying a design student's success on the path to professional designer. A number of synonyms for *creative* actually describe the core energy driving designers and designs towards brilliance. Some of these synonyms are *imaginative*, *resourceful*, *original*, *fertile*, *ingenious*, *inspired*, *inventive*, and *innovative*.

They each recognize that, in achieving good design, pursuit and performance are one. A vibrant path harvests productive capacity.

There is little convincing evidence that individuals described or observed as *creative* are born visionary. In the design disciplines, the common trait of so-called *creative* ones is that they eagerly develop a storehouse of ideas to draw upon, a cache of ideas bred by practicing, by run-throughs. They regularly practice and therefore expand their compilation of design-related thoughts and ideas – they rehearse the design process. By practicing design, by frequently undertaking design drills, they are developing and acquiring ingredients, ready to apply to their design work.

Imagination requires a bank of images to work from. Resourcefulness requires a substantial stockpile of resources from which to draw upon. Originality requires profound familiarity with beginnings and sources. Fertility stems from an array of inputs and nutrients already gathered and on hand. Ingenuity is cultivated by exposing oneself to (and emerging from) a series of challenges that build cleverness. Inspired outcomes require experiencing many notable, inspirational events. Inventiveness results from resolute patterns and habits of

Study of built forms and landscape forms composed of intersecting volumes.

experimentation. And innovation requires gaining experience of methods that stimulate new thinking and new ideas.

This chapter will emphasize how to build the background and resources for new design ideas. It will prepare the groundwork essential to shape imagination, invention, and inspiration. It will provide a map to design discovery, plotting a personalized path to design innovation.

THE LEFT-BRAIN AND RIGHT-BRAIN THEORIES RELATED TO DRAWING

The left-brain and right-brain theories (L+R) have held substantial ground since emerging in the 1960s. These theories have been applied to explanations of how *creativity* operates and unfolds in the production of artistic actions. There is now a substantial body of work that endeavors to understand and guide drawing and design ideation through an L+R brain perspective (Edwards 2012).

Those applying the L+R brain theories to drawing and design hold that the right brain engages drawing activity more intuitively, with less literal results – representing and interpreting things more comprehensively, more meaningfully, and more expressively as whole assemblages of lines, surfaces, shades, and textures. It is held that the left brain interprets visual and conceptual elements logically, arriving at quick, methodical, and less imaginative conclusions – abstract, extra-simple, and symbolized.

The L+R brain theories are now under scrutiny. There remains general agreement that the left- and right-brain hemispheres address and process differing and somewhat distinct categories of thinking. But recent research has suggested that earlier theories of the L+R brain performance have oversimplified the separation of the left- and right-brain functions and outcomes. Analysts now observe complex interrelated and interwoven functions of the left- and right-brain sectors. There is considerable evidence that the two sectors cross over, combine, and interact in back-and-forth exchange processes

14   PREPARING FOR DESIGN DISCOVERY

– sometimes sharing and contributing simultaneously in both physiological and psychological realms.

EXPLICIT VERSUS IMPLICIT KNOWLEDGE

Current research and resulting theories surrounding *creativity* employ new terminology in the quest to explain innovative and inventive behavior and outcomes. Without refuting that the left- and right-brain sectors serve distinct and dominant functions, the emphasis is now on investigating the type of knowledge and thought processes employed – with less focus on the location in the brain where they originate and are processed.

Currently, neurological research concentrates on describing and explaining *creativity* from the perspective of two distinct types of knowledge – explicit knowledge and implicit knowledge.

Explicit knowledge is the grouping and display of useful information, such as in a woodworker's manual on how to build a desk. It informs the woodworker, listing the materials needed and providing step-by-step procedures on processing and assembling the parts into a finished piece of furniture.

Implicit knowledge comprises previously processed and internalized banks of interrelated information based upon experiences, including successes, failures, and preferences. It is a comprehensive and fully fledged thinking-to-action skill set. In the woodworking example, implicit knowledge is compiled and stored within the experienced woodworker over many years and many projects. It is the reservoir of implicit knowledge that steers the master to fashion and produce a desk autonomously. The end result is crafted with confidence, distinguished by its high quality.

But the key is that explicit knowledge was essential to the formation of the master woodworker's implicit knowledge. Explicit knowledge incrementally packs together and becomes the capability of the master woodworker, eventually amassed to form implicit knowledge that drives the master's work. Explicit knowledge builds the master and leads to mastery.

It is therefore important to engage actively in piece-by-piece preparation (explicit knowledge build-up) in order to assemble a complex of implicit knowledge that yields exceptional design results. Implicit knowledge is cultivated by practicing the act of design – through routine exercises. Calisthenic and gymnastic exercises produce competitive performance in athletes. Similarly, the practice of drawing produces visual and spatial fitness that feeds excellence

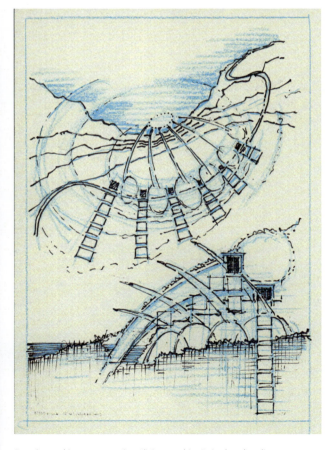

Experimental image portraying "living machine" sited at shoreline.

16 PREPARING FOR DESIGN DISCOVERY

in design. An active program of drawing, for the purpose of practice, is vital to generating fresh and well-balanced design ideas.

DESIGN *EXPERIMENTS* DIFFER FROM DESIGN *EXPLORATIONS*

The drawing exercises in each chapter of this book progress from *experimental* types (i.e. those not applied to real sites or real projects) to *explorations* (i.e. those directly applied and related to real project design work).

Science and mathematics use the expression *experimentation* to describe the testing of a question (a hypothesis). The testing proceeds with clear and reproducible methods. The results of experiments are charted and compared for consistency. Often these experiments dramatically simplify a real-world condition, and implement the *experiment* in laboratory or clinical confines.

In the realm of drawing and design, *experimentation* is similar, but with a greater emphasis on questioning than answering Drawing *experiments* are not so controlled. They are productive when they bring about unanticipated results – results that stimulate more pondering, more questioning. Experimental drawings concentrate on the enjoyable process of seeking, not seriously driven to find "the answer." Drawing experiments are successful when they generate curiosity, evoke more questions, and suggest alternative routes to a design idea. Drawing-based *experiments* operate freely. They are not confined within many parameters. They are not bound to formulaic procedures. Looking for design ideas through *experimentation* provides useful speculations that may lead to new possibilities – possibilities freed from preconceptions, even though their applicability is yet to be determined. These *experiments* endeavor to deliver fresh and unforeseen spatial ideas beyond the boundaries typically set by real projects.

Exploration in the sciences, math, medicine, and data analysis deals with finding answers typically within real and existing situations. For instance, *exploration* when applied to discovery within a broad and expansive existing collection of data is frequently termed *data*

PREPARING FOR DESIGN DISCOVERY   17

mining. This term establishes the primary distinction between *experimentation* and *exploration*. *Exploration* digs into real settings, endeavoring to pull out or extract concrete patterns, interpretations, answers – that is, solutions.

Drawing and design *explorations* address considerations that are specific to a project. *Explorations* employ drawings to discover and suggest potential design solutions fitting a particular site, program, client, and contextual parameters. An *exploration*, however, is not responsible to reveal detailed design solutions. Similar to design *experiments*, design *explorations* produce results without being presupposed. *Explorations* are set on a particular path of discovery. They are carried out keyed into tangible conditions that are to be addressed in a specific landscape design task. *Explorations* strive to generate design ideas, expanding the array of project-specific design alternatives. They expand a design process by uncovering novel and workable real-world solutions.

Design *experimentation* employs a relaxed, recreational, curious, and questioning drawing process that generates surprising, even delightful, graphic images. Images resulting from an *experiment* are imaginative and primal. They are served up and witnessed for the very first time. On one hand, they are whimsical, yet at the same time they are valuable design discoveries. *Experimental* images should be viewed and cataloged design ideas, design prospects. Since *experimental* design ideas are not based in real-project or real-site circumstances, they generate form on vacation, without

Design experiment introducing negative space corridors to a field of forms.

function tagging along. They pose no particular spatial bearing or alignment. They produce graphic images that are original, free to be interpreted from multiple vantage points. In landscape design an *experimental* image, though often first viewed as a conceptual diagram, *parti*, or plan diagram, should be simultaneously viewed and queried as if it is a site section, an elevation, an object, a space, or even a visual representation of environmental systems.

Design *explorations* have similarities to experiments in that they venture into relatively uncharted territory, but *explorations* develop imagery that is more considerate of actual space and landscapes. Design *explorations* dig for ideas within drawings that address tangible sites and settings. *Explorations* proceed with a greater sense of responsibility to real conditions. They deal with more constraints, variables, and details – such as forces of gravity, landform configurations, existing negative and positive spatial elements, and structural integrity. *Explorations* devote increased attention to pragmatic and functional aspects necessarily integrated with real-world design work.

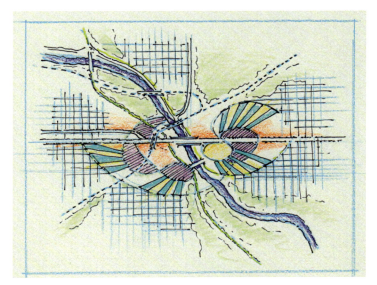

Design exploration visualizing modifications to land use and forms at city edge, applied to adaptive reuse of abandoned industrial sites.

PREPARING FOR DESIGN DISCOVERY 19

PARAMETERS FOR THE EXERCISES (CHAPTERS 1 THROUGH 5)

Experiments and *explorations*, though differing in approaches and outcomes, are both indispensable design ideation exercises. Chapters 1 through 5 each conclude with drawing exercises that help design students and professionals utilize design discovery principles that are discussed in the essays that open each chapter. This book is lesson-centered, providing its greatest value when the chapter-end exercises are fulfilled straight away, immediately after considering the themes presented in the essays.

The exercises offer the reader direct and simple drawing-based methods to translate design thoughts into imagery. Following along and fulfilling each exercise promptly will deliver rewards. Personal drawing styles will relax, become agile, and be motivated with anticipation for discovering ideas. The exercises are formed to find ideas without any expectation or concern for the images being "art" or "artistic." The process will produce a rewarding sense of design recreation – a breather from any notion that design is work. Look ahead for the enjoyment, and delight in the surprises.

While carrying out these exercises, welcome a sense of lightness. Think of each exercise as a brief retreat. Approach each as a simple event, an expression of freedom, a frisky rehearsal, a bit of a romp. Be free of concerns for achieving a grand performance. Consider the simplicity and purity of drawing. It provides the path for an idea to become imagined, to become an image. Enjoy the release of a visual thought, letting it travel the path of brain, arm, elbow, wrist, and fingers – into pen and onto paper. Celebrate drawing as a wholesome and clear design communication technology. Appreciate spontaneous aspects of drawing and enjoy some release offered by improvisation. Draw playfully, practicing design ideas that just may be spot on.

[Note: The drawing exercises provided in this book employ foundational drawing and sketching skills. These design-drawing exercises employ simple representational sketching of places,

20   PREPARING FOR DESIGN DISCOVERY

spaces, and objects (real and imagined), using intuitive perspective methods. Experimental drawing methods will also be used, such as contour-surface drawing and positive–negative space drawing techniques.]

THE METHODS AND MEDIA FOR DRAWING EXERCISES

The methods and media recommended for most of the follow-along exercises are familiar and time tested. The exercise outcomes will be most successful when using a high-quality sketchbook, a non-photo blue pencil, and a few black ink pens of one's preference (offering varied line weights from extra-fine to medium). Accompany the exercises with a folded piece of cardstock paper or postcard that remains tucked in the sketchbook, serving as a handy straight-edge for use when desired. The cardstock edge yields informal straight lines – casual and more suited to sketching.

The exercises can be best fulfilled by using high-quality sketchbooks with stiff ivory paper. Ideal is a sketchbook that is comfortable for drawing while held in hand, or set across one's leg or the lap while sitting. Throughout this book the sketchbook sizes vary, based on the exercise. Recommendations are made in the instructions for each exercise. Generally, while following through with the exercises in this book, be prepared with sketchbooks in the following sizes: small (e.g. 13 × 21 cm; 5.1 × 8.3 in); medium (e.g. 19 × 25 cm; 7.3 × 9.8 in); and large (e.g. 21 × 30 cm; 8.5 × 11.8 in).

High-quality sketchbooks of ivory paper aid the purposes of the exercises. The off-white background brings substance to the drawing field. Landscape environments rarely exist in pure white fields. Generally neutral tones compose a majority of all landscape settings. Therefore, an ivory drawing medium provides the sensation of a space filled with ingredients and atmosphere of a landscape, before a sketch even begins.

[Note: The exploration-style exercises in the later chapters produce more complex and comprehensive drawings. They employ color

Design exploration imagining art structure catching rain, conveyed to wetland basin.

rendering on single-sheet, neutral-tone art papers, not necessarily available in sketchbooks.]

In the exercises, the combined use of non-photo blue pencils followed by black ink-pen overlay is deliberate. Drawing exercises aimed at searching for design ideas must be free to evolve and transform fluidly. To keep the process flowing, an unrestrained and continuous drawing style is needed. A pale-blue pencil provides a calm, loose and relaxing medium for introducing lines and shapes on paper. The blue lines attract less judgment as right or wrong than inked lines seem to. Light pencil lines are wonderfully temporary and invite change and adjustments. They look and seem malleable. The initial blue lines meet paper with an attitude of searching and sampling. This technique causes the first sketch gestures to remain comfortable and experimental, appearing impermanent or unfixed. This keeps a drawing exercise on its target of practicing design – rather than designing.

PREPARING FOR DESIGN DISCOVERY

The blue-line session is short, just a few moments. Its purpose is marking the paper, expecting a design springboard to appear. Effectively, the blank sketch page is not the starting point for a successful design exercise. This is an important distinction. For these exercises, the start lies in the skeleton of blue lines arranged on the sketch page instantaneously. The simple blue lines can be considered imaginary. They are unassuming marks that provide the exercise with a fruitful point of departure. The marks are caricatures of what may soon suggest a fresh look at space and form.

[Note: The non-photo blue pencil marks serve to form a jump-start for each drawing exercise. But as a technique, it also provides useful benefits in reproduction of the drawing outcomes. Copying and scanning technologies can be adjusted to eliminate reading the non-photo blue pencil lines and tones. This allows for reproductions that portray only the inked lines and tones. Conversely, copying and scanning technologies can be adjusted to read and even amplify the blue-line aspects of a sketch or design diagram. This affords reproduction options where the ink lines and blue pencil lines are captured together, transformed into gray-scale images with richness and depth.]

With the pencil lines providing a start, a foundation, the exercise process now invites black ink to join the visual conversation and design discovery process. The exercise proceeds in a manner familiar to designers, with ink committed to express and give permanence to an image, a visual idea. Continuing with quick pace and a sense of immediacy, ink lines, tones, and textures begin to claim and occupy space in the drawing. Ink lines take their place beside and upon the loosely fixed blue-line elements. The exercise finds substance in the ink layers, finishing straight way with no fret. The inking phase resolves on its own rather quickly. An outcome is born. It appears without being predicted. The conclusion emerges without being driven by visual templates from before.

An exercise is just that – an exercise. It produces a tangible visual outcome. The resulting diagram or drawing now has its place in the universe of design possibilities. The exercises are brief. This builds excitement to engage in another round or two while the sketchbook, pencils, and pens are at hand. The more often these exercises are performed, anticipating new design ideas and discoveries, the more likely the results – fresh and useful design ideas – will be retained for future recall.

[Note: Images produced in any drawing exercise should be revisited, immediately upon completion, or soon, or later. Regardless if the exercise is an experiment or exploration, results should not be put away as conclusive or final. Images produced in an exercise are very useful for extended consideration, additional learning, and more discoveries. Remember that the drawings resulting from any exercise are personally invented; they are original. This means they are very valuable as visual ideas, ripe to enhance and refine. They may also become a very important starting point for a new exercise, a new experiment or exploration. Exercise results frequently in diagrammatic imagery, readily eliciting site plan interpretations. To take full advantage of exercise results, view them from many different perspectives, such as representing: landscape section and elevation images; or three-dimensional objects like environmental art forms in landscape settings; or plans portraying forms applied to extensive regional landscapes.]

Design-drawing exercises "draw out" and "draw upon" memories – memories that are visual, spatial, and design-related. The exercises in this book simultaneously engage stored and momentary memories of the designer. The memories that are accessed while drawing may already be resident in the designer's psyche (long-term or short-term forms). Some memories are incidental, immediate impressions, fleeting sensory memories (Penfield 1952). Rarely are memories stored in the brain in complete packages, like books on a shelf. But the sketchbook records and stores the evidence of the array of memories tapped while fulfilling the exercise. The exercise conclusion is a drawing that has assembled a new memory – a new consideration for design. The sketchbook "remembers" the design experiment or exploration, making it ever available for future review and application.

DESIGN AEROBICS EXERCISES – FRAME-TO-FRAME

[Note: If not already studied, review the "Parameters for the exercises" and "Methods and media" sections above before commencing the exercises.]

A study of form, exploring co-housing cluster framed in a landscape hosting intensive agriculture and habitat restoration.

These exercises utilize a frame-to-frame format promoting an evolution of images. This technique calls for loosely redrawing the previous frame but freeing the next drawing to transform or change. Changes or shifts occur in simple ways. Variations result by way of uncomplicated choices, such as adding, subtracting, reforming, and deforming the prior image. These step-by-step exercises use simple lines, shapes, and tones. They generate diagrammatic images and are meant to discover visual clues from which design ideas are born.

The exercises arrange sequential images side-by-side and frame-to-frame. Each exercise, each drawing series, uses one sketchbook page. A small sketchbook works well. The number of frames, or steps, for each exercise varies. The successive drawing method encourages spontaneous images. By employing quick, malleable, and changeable sketching techniques, the exercises promote variations that naturally occur while progressing promptly from one drawing to the next. There are no restrictions or limitations on the next drawing. The next drawing should not conform rigidly to its predecessor. It should be free to become "new" through simple modification. Each successive drawing is a new and different image, related to but independent of its previous variation. Each new drawing, or diagram, builds upon some aspect of the previous one, but the new drawing is not confined in any way by what appeared in the previous step.

[Note: Designers are well aware of the valued trace-overly method that is very productive in generating variations of a previous image. These exercises are purposely not using a trace-overly method. Tracing a previous image is used for the purposes of refining, re-dimensioning, and quality improvement of the image beneath. These exercises are not for the purpose of refining or improving the previous image. In fact, the side-by-side, frame-to-fame method is purposely helping the designer break away from minor modifications and fix-it responsibilities. The side-by-side method allows the next drawing – the next modification – to be fresh, new, and unconstrained by the previous version.]

ROUND ROBIN

This exercise originates by drawing a series of simple frames on one sketchbook page. The frames represent an existing neutral space. The first frame provides a base area, a blank slate. It imposes no restraints – a limitless platform from which to begin an *experiment*.

This exercise uses one sketchbook page holding six frames. Plan ahead by drawing the empty – roughly equally proportioned – frames on a sketchbook page (use a blue pencil). Establishing the frames with the cardstock straight-edge is helpful. This honors the experiment with a sense of craft. The two examples of this exercise illustrate the sequential arrangement of the frames (see the two example figures). The arrows in each example indicate the progression from the first to the sixth frame.

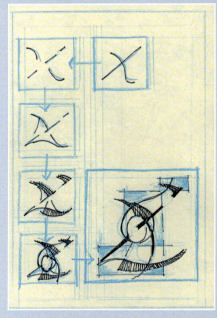

Round robin – Example 1: Six-step frame-to-frame design experiment (beginning with two intersecting lines).

The final (sixth) frame is larger. In the examples, it is double the size of each of the first five. Preparing the final frame larger than the others provides the exercise with an end point. The enlarged final frame affords an opportunity to illustrate a conclusion, summarizing cause-and-effect changes that modified the previous stages. The final frame becomes a wrap-up, visualizing an intervention in an imagined space, drawn with more detail and substance than the earlier, developmental frames.

With little forethought, the first frame invites a drawing composed of a few lines or shapes (start with the blue pencil). The first drawing becomes the originator. Think of the image as expressing some spatial conditions – such as an extant object or two, or symbols of natural forces (wind, water, light, etc.). Or think of the initial marks more abstractly, as simple geometric patterns or vectors suggesting movement that is present in a space. Then, step-by-step, additional frames are drawn, drawing iterations. A progression of associated imagery appears, moving around the sketchbook page. Each successive frame builds from the previous one – expanding, moving, and growing into

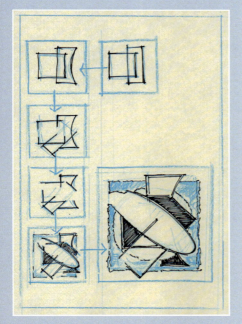

Round robin – Example 2: Six-step frame-to-frame design experiment (beginning with two intersecting closed shapes).

a sequence of related but ever-evolving visual expressions.

To stimulate change and evolution from one frame to the next, introduce simple means to cause the next diagram to alter or adapt. Variations on the previous image are readily achieved by engaging combinations of additive and subtractive sketching. Variations can also be achieved by bending or warping the previous drawing using push, pull, and stretch modifications. Be at ease, introducing influences and subtle forces that effect transformation from frame-to-frame. Invite change to affect each new step – changes that compel shifts in patterns and cause geometries to interact or intermingle in new ways. Remember that there are no wrong methods or wrong results in an exercise of this kind. Simply keep changing the image in the next frame by drawing a variant of the previous one.

Upon fulfilling the start-frame and a subsequent four-frame sequence, a design image, a design idea, is ready to build which concludes the exercise. The conclusion formulates a more detailed image adapted from the fourth variation. As mentioned, the examples illustrate the final step being performed within a larger frame than the earlier ones. The final frame summons closure and completion. While proceeding quickly, the final frame becomes a more complex, more elaborate image that is derived from forms drawn in the previous frames (mostly the fourth frame). The image in the final frame is developed with more substance (tone and texture, with more varied line weights). The final frame is a synthesis composed from earlier images. In the final diagram, enjoy adding a few more details that interpret landscape-relevant aspects. Visualize and translate the image to express a sense of depth and three dimensions. Add more tone, texture, and elements that might suggest the diagram responding to landform and vegetative systems. The exercise, the experiment, has reached a point of closure. A prospective design idea has been generated.

MOVE, MERGE, AND MINGLE

This exercise is similar to "Round robin," but achieves an experiment in three larger frames arranged in a row, side-by-side (see the example figure). As before, use the blue pencil to approximate the lines and shapes to develop a base image in frame one. Utilize the blue pencil initially to develop the images in frames two and three as well.

Start in frame one by drawing a number of closed shapes. Once the shapes are drawn, quickly determine a direction in which each shape will move, intending that they *move* toward and merge with each other. Indicate these directions with arrows drawn with blue pencil in the first frame.

The second frame will express an outcome of the shapes moving and *merging*, becoming more integrated and interrelated. Proceed immediately to draw the results of the movement, producing a merging of the shapes in frame two. The example illustrates the shapes yielding to each other, interlocking and giving up some volume to fit together as a group – a family of forms.

Next, briefly observe the configuration that has resulted from the merging of the shapes in frame two. Look for and quickly commit to an ordering system expressed by two intersecting axes. Draw these axes through and over the shapes in frame two. The example illustrates two axes drawn (in frame two)

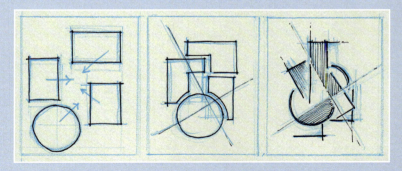

Move, merge, and mingle: Three-step, frame-to-frame design experiment (beginning with four closed shapes).

orthogonally related to each other. In the example the origin of the axes relates somewhat to the directions set for the shapes to move from frame one to frame two. In this experiment, the determination of two axes is a personal decision; it need not follow the example here.

Finally, the outcome of frame three will address the concept of *mingle*. Re-establish the two axes from frame two in frame three. Then begin drawing a result, an event, in which the four merged shapes are imagined to engage each other more deeply, to collaborate. Imagine the shapes mingling with each other. The two axes provide a basis (order and directions) for the shapes to integrate even more so than they did in step two. In frame three, the shapes become less rigid, more intimate, and more involved with each other. This third step supposes each shape to open up. Portions of each shape are freed to split and detach from its original closed state.

As before, use blue pencil first in frame three. Draw notions of each shape opening up, portions of each shape splitting and moving away from the parent shape, while moving to meet other shapes. Take advantage of the axes to guide the experiment. Sketching with the blue pencil, draw segments of each shape sliding beside, past, and through other portions of other shapes. Allow several portions of the shapes to intersect with each other. Once there are some initial blue-line expressions of the mingling, commit them in ink. The segments of the shapes will evidence that they have circulated, interspersed, and fused into one united and blended form.

At this closing stage, as with the earlier exercise, use the blue pencil and ink pen to add more tone, texture, and features that aid in representing the third frame as a spatial diagram.

MIGRATION

This exercise presents similar goals and objectives noted in the previous two experiments. However, it comprises just two steps. Once one is familiar with design experiments that transpose a base drawing, through multiple steps, culminating in design expression, a two-step or three-step process is often most productive. An example of this abbreviated frame-to-frame venture is provided. As before, use the blue pencil to approximate the lines and shapes to develop a base image in step one, then its translation in step two.

Start in frame one by drawing a number of closed shapes, this time established at the outset in strong axial relationships with each other. The example illustrates four closed shapes that are already merged, interwoven, and tightly interrelated with each other. Notice that the frame itself is not as strict as in the earlier exercises: the shapes extend slightly outside the frame at two points. Once the shapes are drawn, determine the direction in which each shape will move along each axis. Indicate the anticipated movement with blue-pencil arrows. Since the theme of this experiment is migration, imagine the movement as rotational, orbital, and vacillating.

After inking the axes and shapes in the first frame, generate the design idea in the second frame at once, with little deliberation. In frame two, migrate the axes and redraw them in their new rotated relationship to the shapes and frame. Then imagine the shapes each freed from their closed form, section by section drifting to realign and relocate in frame two, based upon the movement vectors set in frame one. In this experiment, add additional sensations of migration by releasing the frame to loosen, to drift, and to interact with the shapes, lines, and forms that are fluctuating as the image evolves and takes form. Allow this experiment to close promptly in frame two. Permit your drawing methods to be free and unbound by such questions as "What should it look like? Where should this shape be drawn?" Instead, just keep drawing – blue pencil then black ink. Move ahead, closing the experiment in the second frame, propelled with an attitude of wonder and a simple declaration that "Something surprising is happening here."

As with the previous experiments, close out this frame using the blue pencil and ink pen to enhance the image by adding more characteristics (tone, texture, etc.) that evoke qualities associated with designed spaces and landscapes.

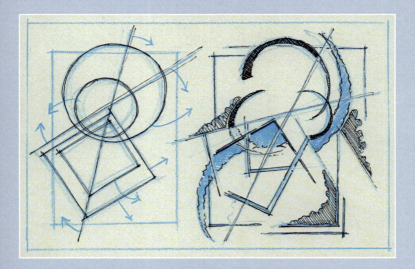

Migration: Two-step frame-to-frame design experiment (beginning with four clustered and overlapping shapes pre-aligned with two axes).

32 PREPARING FOR DESIGN DISCOVERY

REFLECTIONS ON THE DRAWING EXPERIMENTS

Take a moment to consider these questions and reflect:

1. Did you enjoy the freedom granted by inventing an image then effortlessly manipulating new variations, just because you could?
2. Did you experience some refreshing moments as one drawing changed to another without much thought or effort?
3. Did you appreciate the simple act of discovery as your drawings progressed, changed, and altered in rather unpredictable ways?
4. Were you able to sense that the sequential images could in some way suggest designs or imaginary spaces taking form amid a landscape of drawing?
5. Were you able to reduce your sense of control over the visual patterns, allowing the imagery to have a say in where the next line, tone, or gesture appeared (or disappeared)?
6. Did you begin to discover opportunities just to relax, stretch, and enjoy – to walk-and-talk visually with your mind, your eyes, your hand, and your sketchbook without many interruptions from judgments and critiques?
7. Could you see yourself enjoying frequent *conversations* with these visual experiments – entertaining a light question-and-answer dialogue with diagrams and images as you. your pencils, pens, and sketchbook make them appear?
8. As you sequenced through each design experiment, did you sense a transformation from explicit to implicit (design) knowledge?

These design experiments oversimplify site design and the complexities of design typically managed in landscape architectural projects. Recall that an experiment strives to discover yet untried and unusual possibilities that *just might* contribute to the resolution of complex design challenges. Previously uncharted forms, patterns, geometries, and ordering systems, once discovered, provide a cache of possibilities. Design exercises generate original design ideas for future consideration. Increasing the discovery and cataloging of design possibilities is fostered by regularly and consistently breaking away from the familiar to enjoy and fulfill design experiments. Personalize and adapt these examples of experiments to formulate frequent design recreation outings of your own – practice design, practice design.

REFERENCES

Edwards, B. *Drawing on the Right Side of the Brain: The Definitive Edition.* New York: J.P. Tarcher/Penguin Group, 2012.

Penfield, W. Memory Mechanisms. *AMA Archives of Neurology and Psychiatry*, Vol. 67 (February 1952): 178–198.

FORMS RESPONDING TO SYSTEMS

2

Synopsis: This chapter provides historical background regarding environmental design theory. The roles of form and function in driving design ideas and design interventions are examined. The discourse highlights landscapes as intricate, composed of varied systems – interactive, receptive, and reciprocal. The chapter concludes with form-finding exercises. The drawing experiments acknowledge dynamic attributes at work on a site.

Diagrammatic image exploring hydrologic and atmospheric movements interacting with vegetative and soils systems.

FORMS RESPONDING TO SYSTEMS   35

> **Primary learning outcomes:** By the end of this chapter, students will be able to generate and draw experimental forms informed by the natural and cultural processes that are active on most sites (e.g. wind, topography, hydrology, solar energy, movement patterns, etc.). From these experiments, students will develop diagrammatic forms that express compatibility with and receptivity to other site-related processes. Students will be able to generate and assess the appropriateness of unique and experimentally revealed forms, identifying design interventions that are synergetic, interceding carefully amid complex and sensitive processes.
>
> **Relevance to landscape architectural students and professionals:** The landscape architectural profession is benevolent. It is committed to fitting human needs to the land in ways that sustain and support natural systems, free to perform their life-giving role, both functionally and aesthetically. Broadening the scope of form language that may be applied to site design enhances the preparedness of landscape architects to contribute new ideas in support of this commitment.

FORM *FOLLOWS* FUNCTION + FORM *AS* FUNCTION + FUNCTION *IS* FORM

In 1886 Louis Sullivan coined – and endeavored to establish for all designers – the truism that *form ever follows function*. Sullivan's position was popularized – albeit partially misapplied – when truncated to *form follows function*. This suggests a cause-and-effect association – function does or should cause form. However, the shortening of the phrase did not fully express Sullivan's position. He did not narrowly assert function to be the *only* starting point for every design. Rather, he was addressing a timely concern. In his view, architectural design was serving a very narrow sphere of clients and users. This trend was allowing designs and designers to be excessively engaged in, and even governed by, artistic inclinations and aesthetic favorites.

Sullivan's original phrasing – *form ever follows function* – involves a subtle expression of bond and balance. He cautioned that the

Sketch of green sea turtles, noticing carapace and flipper forms uniting in fluid movement, suspension, and glide.

functional performance requirements for a good design should not be compromised by an arbitrary form. Rather, he felt that form and function must be mutually considered. Sullivan held that good design supports a fluid relationship between form and function, but that function should lead the way when judging the fit of any design decision.

Sullivan maintained that considerable learning is available just by observing objects, nature, and natural phenomena – living creatures and inert objects in nature. Studying these elements in the environment, aided by drawing them, provides a lens better to understand *form*. The process of sketching these features reveals the inborn relationship and interdependence between form and function. Studying the bonds between form and function significantly enriches and improves the design process. Sullivan championed this perspective.

FORMS RESPONDING TO SYSTEMS 37

Sketch of conch shell, recording spiral growth development as form determinant.

The context surrounding his creed is found in Sullivan's full quote:

> Whether it be the sweeping eagle in his flight, or the open apple-blossom, the toiling work-horse, the blithe swan, the branching oak, the winding stream at its base, the drifting clouds, over all the coursing sun, form ever follows function, and this is the law. Where function does not change, form does not change. The granite rocks, the ever-brooding hills, remain for ages; the lightning lives, comes into shape, and dies, in a twinkling.

38   FORMS RESPONDING TO SYSTEMS

> It is the pervading law of all things organic and inorganic, of all things physical and metaphysical, of all things human and all things superhuman, of all true manifestations of the head, of the heart, of the soul, that the life is recognizable in its expression, that form ever follows function. This is the law.
>
> (Sullivan 1922: 408)

Sullivan's law has been misinterpreted by many. He did not pose this truism to limit or subjugate the development of design forms. But whether intended by Sullivan, or by those overreacting to his law, *form follows function* dropped a heavy stone on the freedom of form to contribute equally in a design process.

FORMS ARE VALUES – VALUES ENGAGE SYSTEMS

It is also valuable to consider form and function from the perspective of a less object-oriented design discipline, such as landscape architecture. The landscape architect and environmental planner Ian McHarg demanded that *form must follow more than just function*; form must respect the natural environment in which it is placed. McHarg's enduring charge to designers is serious, pointed. He demands that all decisions – from landscape planning to site design – are obligated to manage form and function empirically, filtered through sound environmental and social-science-based criteria. With this position, he established the foundation for evidence-based design. From his *systems* vantage point, emphasizing natural systems as the fund of all life, forms are – or should be – shaped by the complex interactions among multiple systems. This is a very different perspective than *form follows function*.

From a landscape planning perspective, McHarg teaches that development – alterations to the land – result from values, and those values generate physical forms that manipulate critical patterns. Some of the resulting patterns may be good and carefully supportive. Others are disruptive. And some are adversarial and defiant, scourge-like, clearly destructive. McHarg continuously

FORMS RESPONDING TO SYSTEMS 39

warns that designs implemented in the landscape intervene; they are interventions. They risk interference with the purpose and function of the land. The term *design intervention* announces caution and concern. To some, *design intervention* may imply intrusion. *Intervention* may even connote insensitive, disruptive, and degrading impacts, counterproductive performances. There may be claims that *interventions* disable a site's productive systems, that they are *impositions*, imposing illness on the land.

McHarg draws attention to an axiom that emerged in the eighteenth century – that natural systems are the best designers. This adage can be credited to the birth of applied ecology, where aesthetics in the landscape were modeled after nature's own designs. This historic shift in values shaped a new tradition for what became the profession of landscape architecture. At that time, especially in England, the imposing forms and rigid geometries of the Renaissance were abandoned by landscape architects (garden designers) who believed that nature and humankind could – and should – form a unified whole. This tradition, or trend, led to landscape designs that favored the look of nature. In *Design with Nature* McHarg describes – and partially praises – this new tradition as follows: "The ruling principle was that 'nature is the gardener's best designer' – an empirical ecology" (McHarg 1992: 73).

McHarg notes that design sentiment turned against the so-called artificial walled garden as "nature." This introduced the science of ecology as a design force, shaping landscapes and forming attitudes that highly valued the natural environment. The new forms of gardens became truer models of the scope and breadth of nature.

> The meadow was the single artifice – the remaining components were natural expressions, their dramatic and experiential qualities exploited, it is true, but deriving in the first place from that observed in nature . . .

Nature itself produced the aesthetic; the simple geometry – not simplicity but simple-mindedness of the Renaissance was banished. "Nature abhors a straight line."

(McHarg 1992: 73)

The aesthetics driving these designers' landscape preferences developed not only from observations of nature, but were also based on a diversification of world-view, especially in the Orient, where asymmetry was revered, a signature dwelling in natural orders. "In the 18th century landscape began the revolution that banished

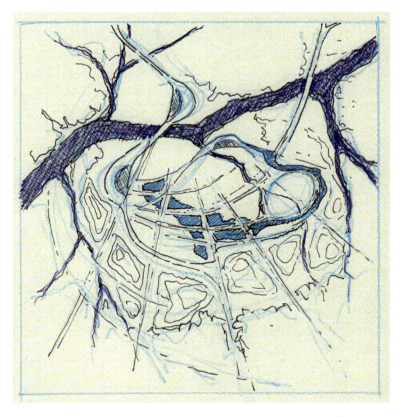

Design experiment imagining a village form responding to site hosting oxbow wetlands and high stream density flowing into on-site river.

the classical image and imposition of its geometry as a symbol of man-nature" (McHarg 1992: 73).

It is interesting that McHarg himself may have reacted to a misattributed version of Sullivan's axiom. As he nicely concludes by restating and elaborating on Sullivan's true stance in the following:

> This tradition is important in many respects. It founded applied ecology as a basis for function and aesthetics in the landscape. Indeed, before the manifesto of modern architecture had been propounded – "form follows function" – it had been superseded by the 18th century concept, in which form and process were indivisible aspects of a singular phenomenon . . .
>
> (McHarg 1992: 73)

> Another reason for [this tradition's] importance lies in the fact that it was a creation. Here landscape architects, like the empiricist doctor, found a land in ill health and brought it to good heart and to beauty. Man the artist, understanding nature's laws and forms, accelerated the process of regeneration so well indeed that who today can discern the artifice from the untouched? Nature completed man's work.
>
> (McHarg 1992: 74)

McHarg helps designers grasp that the eighteenth-century naturalized gardens were applying a nature-teacher design model. This shift remains a vital component of contemporary design, endeavoring to generate sustainable landscapes. This eighteenth-century tradition introduced nature-compassionate landscape forms, even in highly manipulated landscapes. McHarg counsels landscape architects that nature will provide subtle and gentle wisdom. That with attentiveness to nature, natural systems, and the symbiotic inner workings (functions) of sites, life-giving forms and patterns for landscapes are discovered. Sensitively engaging the nature informant as a unifying hinge point between *form* and *function* teaches designers how to design and build. This approach results in

42 FORMS RESPONDING TO SYSTEMS

places that fit, born out of an equitable, reciprocal, and generative nature–human ecology.

> The rejection of nature as crude, vile – the lapsed paradise – and the recognition of the land as the milieu of life, which could be made rich and fair, is the great volte face of the western world . . . indeed it succumbed to an excess of romanticism . . . but it was a precursory ecology, its practitioners were more perceptive and capable than its theorist advocates. And it has endured.
>
> (McHarg 1992: 74)

McHarg's primary purpose in *Design with Nature* is to establish a thorough landscape planning decision-making methodology, placing natural systems (ecology) in the position to form landscape plans that restore and cure. The scale of form he addresses is mostly expansive and multi-site in scope. He establishes a new guardian for nature–human interventions that far outdistances the chiefly bucolic eighteenth-century value that authorized nature to prevail as landscape designer.

McHarg does not accuse form of being a delinquent, or a villain, provided the proper conscience drives design. He does not hold that form must take a back seat to function. Indeed, he understands that carefully rendered form enriches and contributes useful functions to the landscape and its users. He clearly signals that form will not be fulfilled if required ever to bow to function. In fact, he illustrates that form and function are not independent players, but partners that are vigorously arranged within a community of interrelated systems.

For landscape architects engaging site design, McHarg's regional-scale notions are transferable. His insights urge innovation in the search for design solutions, versatile and responsive forms applied to landscape interventions. Nature illuminates bright and benevolent forms in which nature and humanity collaborate. These forms are

FORMS RESPONDING TO SYSTEMS 43

Experimental drawing visualizing a flexible spatial order emulating fish-like fluidity.

44   FORMS RESPONDING TO SYSTEMS

innate companions with dynamic interlocking systems, composed by the fund of life. McHarg substantiates the role of experimentation in design, confirming that sciences are exploratory and experimental processes, and key to *inform*ing best fit and good design. "Form then is communication, the presentation of meaning" (McHarg 1992: 169).

Natural and social ecologies express robust and stirring systems of matter, energies, attitudes, life forces, and life spaces. Designs introduced in the land must communicate with these vigorous forces. The forms must be responsive to, combine with, and befriend these lively systems. A good design, a worthy intervention, earns an invitation to be an insider. The forms employed are necessarily agile, supple, nimble, permeable, mutable – readily transformable. They achieve membership as co-workers in making vital spaces and places.

A core purpose of landscape architectural design is to form spaces that sustain, support the resident natural and social systems – those systems operating in, on, and around the site. The best of these spaces are programmed to afford access to nature (or replicas of pieces of nature). They frequently provide rooms for life forms and communities (both natural and human) to occupy and experience. The spaces are often hosting carefully positioned structures for respite – networked together by systems of passages – achieving such within a forum of beauty and delight.

FREEING FORM – FOR A WHILE

It may be popular to charge Sullivan as a design process legislator. Some interpret that he insisted function is always first, followed by form – that the eagle needed to fly and therefore wings followed. McHarg reacted to the *form follows function* paradigm that is commonly attributed to Sullivan. But he shaped his planning and design treatises from a quite different perspective. He saw environmental and social systems, the sciences, as the hub – the genesis for design. He held that design processed through the sciences simultaneously

FORMS RESPONDING TO SYSTEMS

generates form and function – form is function, and function is form. McHarg's phrasing would be *the eagle, flight, and its wings became together – before wings there was no eagle.*

A discussion of form and function should not overwhelm or confound the joy of designing. Sullivan, McHarg, and others wrestled with questions about form, function, and design. However, they did not intend the design process to be paralyzed in the query. Designs naturally begin in an experimental, exploratory environment. Designing needs a warm-up period, considering design possibilities early on. Moving around the form–function arena for a while allows us to appreciate the complexities, the synergies, that serve a site's productive natural, social, and cultural systems.

The profession acknowledges that a design intervention must carefully join a site, respecting the productive and sometimes

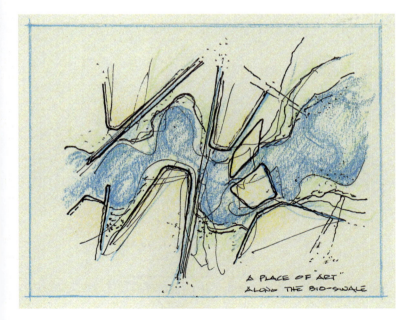

Design experiment imagining artistic structures interacting with and slowing storm water movement through a bio-swale channel.

sensitive processes it hosts. An alternative term, declaring what landscape architects introduce into sites, should be design *intercessions*. Interceding is a compassionate and partnering action, intent on unification. It is the act of pleading on one's behalf, typically for the purpose of settling a disagreement or dispute. It harbors the notion of negotiating differences with an outcome that sustains essential balance for all players involved – a collective stability, equilibrium.

Landscapes and their native systems provide landscape architects with clues about shapes, layouts, and arrangements for intercessions that not only fit the site but add fitness and vitality to the community of systems and users sharing the site. The promise of good design is realized when forms (intercessions) positioned in a site are motion sensitive, change worthy, flexible to surprises – productive partners with the natural and social systems, resident and intended.

Design experiments can emphasize the discovery of forms without challenging a particular form–function stance. Endeavoring to reveal

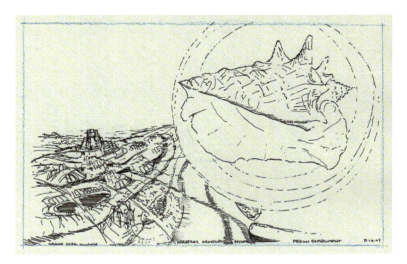

Experimental drawing, expressing patterns of human development, circulation, and landform inspired by attributes of a seashell.

forms that fit well with the land, that intercede rather than intervene, is useful preparation for any design. An act of intercession is a team-building procedure. Experimental drawing is one avenue for producing form ideas that may contribute to a successful design intercession. Forms that exhibit dynamic qualities – forms that may interrelate capably with other dynamic players – are initially uncovered in the act of drawing. Freely applied to the act of finding, drawing is a dynamic, experimental act; it is visual inquiry. The sketchbook provides a malleable arena, ideal in the search for design ideas that are supple and agreeable, ideal for the discovery of forms that are yielding, compliant with lively systems working on and within a site (Lappe 1972).

Landscape architects are very responsible designers. Today, this conscience results in immediate focus on functional requirements, the program, the capacities, the predefined parameters of a project. The following exercises offer a retreat, a recess from the function-first trend. They promote an open search for form and afford simple form-finding techniques, employing diagramming and drawing. They do not address real projects with complex natural, social, or cultural ecologies. They are for the purpose of practicing how to find site-sensitive forms. Then, in the process of rehearsing form-finding, original ideas about form are recorded and stored for application in current and future projects.

Searching for a diverse array of forms (ordering and organizational systems, patterning, geometries, etc.) is more fluid and productive when unbound by the call to serve function first. Granted, design exercises that isolate form-finding are clearly not engaged in holistic design. But, ultimately, proper fulfillment of the functional realm of a project will not be compromised by allowing form to recreate and expand its own possibilities. Design experimentation strengthens the designer's form vocabulary and form voice. Experimentation with form alone prepares opportunities for an enriched union of the form–function blend.

48   FORMS RESPONDING TO SYSTEMS

FORM-FINDING EXERCISES

The following design experiments provide ways to find forms that are sensitive to site systems that are characterized by change and movement. These exercises imagine that there are subtle and strong forces working in and acting upon a site. The forces can be both natural and physical (e.g. wind, water, solar input, gravity, weight, adhesion, leverage, etc.). With sketchbook, pencil, and pen, the exercises diagram forces interacting with forms as they respond to – and are shaped by – various forces. The drawings seek form variants that act cooperatively, becoming process-like rather than fixed and static interruptions. The studies ponder actions, movements, and effects caused by forces, such as rotation, migration, lift, and fall. Hand-drawn experimental images illustrate clues about site patterning and structural orders that tend to yield to and are more symbiotic with a site's natural systems. Of interest is the discovery of form types that ally with natural forces, rather than resist them.

These exercises are free of pragmatic constraints. Active intuition, pencil, pen, and paper are the only things needed to perform the exercises. There are no programmatic requirements for space allocation. There are no defined user needs, no parking-space quotas, no stormwater capacities governing your experiments. There are no assignments to achieve particular performances or "functions." There are no restrictions to finding forms. Simply use diagrammatic drawing techniques to explore, discovering forms and patterns that may interact well with various systems and forces, both natural and cultural.

To start, open the sketchbook to a fresh page. Get pencils and pens ready. Have a cardstock straight-edge handy. These exercises will provide enjoyable sketching time, and design ideas that are worth pondering.

Approach these form-finding experiments much like taking a break from work. Consider the sketching time to be much like catching a short read, advancing a few pages in a book that is captivating and provides retreat. The reading time is enhanced when combined with a favored ritual, like sipping coffee and nibbling on a croissant. Using this analogy, the tactile experiences of sketching are the sip and the bite. The engagement of design thought and ideas while sketching is the short, refreshing read.

The methods and media for the exercises

- These are again frame-to-frame exercises. They work well with three frames on one sketchbook page, from top to bottom (see the examples of the two completed exercises, below). Start by sketching the three frames with a blue pencil.
- Next, invent a "site" in your sketchbook – a simple site, initially in plan view. Provide some topography (contour lines) on the site. Insert the footprint of one or two structures on the site, or start with an undisturbed site. Include vegetation masses and other site features to give the site a sense of reality.
- Next, set within the site some dynamic traits, some forces. Allow these to influence the drawing process. Activate the design experiment. Choose one or two traits from the categories listed below. Or develop others that encourage a design experiment in which forms respond to forces or actions encountered in landscape settings. Allow the traits to interact quickly with the images you sketch. Permit the influences to affect the placement of lines, shapes, and patterns in the design experiment. Acknowledge sketching as a process that can discover forms that sensitively interact and integrate with valued systems and qualities on a site. While sketching, consciously allow the selected traits to become tangible and visual, directly influencing the experimental drawing.

List of traits, qualities, systems, forces

- Partnering action and qualities: linking, joining, moving, sliding, rotating, migrating.
- Adaptability qualities: yielding, malleable, permeable, porous, bending, pliable, flexible.

50   FORMS RESPONDING TO SYSTEMS

- Natural systems or forces: wind (cooling breezes, warming winds), topography, hydrology (surface or ground water), solar energy, diurnal sun-path patterns.
- Cultural/social systems on the site: movement patterns, gathering nodes, territories, viewing points, rest spots.

EXERCISE 1

Three frames
Move this exercise along quickly. To get started, use a blue pencil to scribe three roughly equal frames on a sketchbook page. This experiment works by developing the three frames from top to bottom. Preparing the frames first helps to keep the exercise progressing quickly from start to finish, minimizing pauses and think-before-drawing delays. The example of the completed exercise provides a helpful guide.

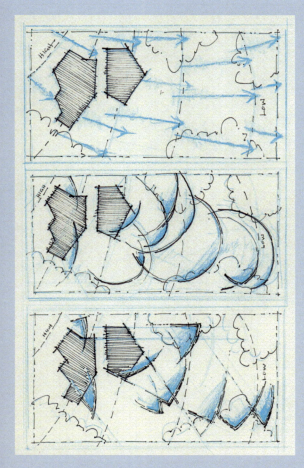

Example of completed Exercise 1.

Frame one

In the top frame, continue with the blue pencil to draft a diagram of a site boundary and some existing conditions that characterize the site. Draw a few contour lines to suggest landform. Determine the high to low elevation trends of the imaginary

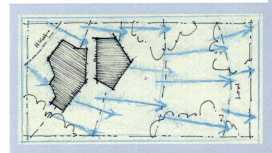

Example of Exercise 1, frame one – representing existing site and site traits.

landform and note them in the drawing. Include some exiting structures or other physical elements that pre-exist in/on the site. Represent building footprints or other structures conventionally. Draw some vegetation masses to provide natural structure on the site.

Frame two

In the second frame, first redraw the site and its characteristics (existing structures, vegetation masses, on-site natural forces, etc.) using a blue pencil. The site information need not be redrawn precisely in frame two. Immediately after redrawing the site, spontaneously sketch

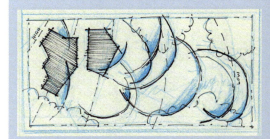

Example of Exercise 1, frame two – representing forms interacting with site traits.

(diagram) lines and shapes that interact with the site's traits. The new lines and shapes represent new conditions (e.g. built elements, landforms, vegetative structures, etc.) that interact with site forces or traits designated in frame one. Activate simple visual thoughts. Quickly transpose those mental images into sketched responses, intermingling with the systems with your pencil and pen. It may be helpful to conceive your traits established in frame one as nature's invisible yet influential traces or fingerprints. The example provided for frame two demonstrates a simple hydrologic pattern (surface water moving in sheet flow downhill) intercepted by arced forms.

Allow the frame two drawing to express the geometries of natural and cultural forces – the directions, movements, and pathways of ephemeral systems. The geometries found in nature are not typically pure Euclidean forms and shapes. They are not perfectly scribed straight lines, circles, squares, rectangles, or triangles. Nature-composed forms often yield to and cooperate with other influences they meet and interact with on the site. They often express pliable geometric qualities, configurations that are asymmetrical, parabolic, arced, or rippled. They may exhibit attributes such as discontinuous yet almost-connected linear strands. The lines and shapes set down in frame two materialize by visualizing and responding to movement vectors, diagrams of forces, directions of gravity, and presence of lift. The drawn images may sense and express reciprocal cycles, such as compression to release.

Frame three

The final frame in this exercise takes advantage of the discoveries in frame two. This step translates the interactive elements sketched in frame two by transforming them into more tangible, buildable expressions. This final step is most productive by simultaneously redrawing the site while adapting notions taken from frame two. So, in frame three, expand and amend the form discoveries sketched in frame two. Express form possibilities, now more tangible in character, by adjusting, adapting, and refining those in frame two. In frame three, review, redraw, and refresh the imagery in frame two by adjusting the geometries and extent of form interventions. Develop the final version in response to "real" site features, both exiting and new (e.g. built elements, landforms, vegetative structures, etc.). In the example provided for frame three, the surface-water detention structures have been modified. The forms have been reduced in scope, and have been unified in their patterning by directly relating to existing geometries on the site (structural footprints).

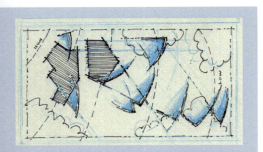

Example of Exercise 1, frame three – transposing the forms in frame two to represent a designed/built landscape.

The example provided for Exercise 1: established a sloping site; introduced a number of built elements; then considered (imagined) the gravity-generated movement of surface water as it progressed downhill in sheet flow. As the experiment proceeded, water was invited to delay in soft-arced interlinking forms, patterned across the site in pliable and communal arrangements. This drawing experiment grasped for and captured a simple idea.

54   FORMS RESPONDING TO SYSTEMS

[Note: As you progress through the book, the exercise instructions will become less prescriptive and less detailed. You are encouraged to read the purpose of each exercise, then review the abbreviated instructions. Next, take note of the sequence and end results of sample images provided for each exercise (design experiment or design exploration). After these preparations, you are free to interpret and modify the exercises to fit your needs. The true value of these exercises, and any you will develop on your own, is that they help you to practice design through drawing without demanding too much time, and without confining you to your current design project assignments.]

EXERCISE 2

The second example of this type of exercise also uses a three-frame sequence (see figure). This experiment also imagines a sloping site, with natural forces working in and on it. The site is represented as a shoreline landform, bordered upslope by a mature woodland. The difference in this experiment is that it views the site interactions and seeks form possibilities by using a section-elevation view (with hints of perspective) in the first and second frames. The exercise then shifts, changing the point of view, looking on to shore from the water body. The final (third) frame also changes the drawing technique, this time visualizing the landscape and form construct using a near-eye-level perspective.

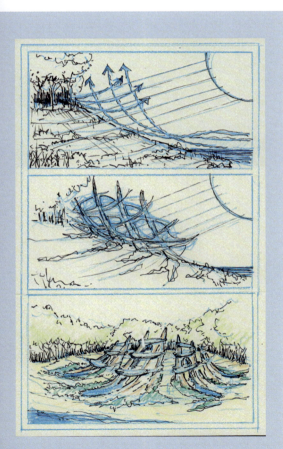

This exercise demonstrates the value of changing the drawing convention used in each step of an experiment (plan view, section and/or elevation, perspective, etc.). Varying the point of view, by using different drawing styles in a single experiment, helps a designer remain sensitive to the three-dimensional spatial nature of landscapes emerging in each image.

Example of completed Exercise 2.

Frame one

In the top frame, quickly consider, then draw, an imaginary site. As before, sketch out the imagined place using a blue pencil, then commit to its characteristics and traits with ink. The example provided illustrates a shoreline landform

Example of Exercise 2, frame one – representing a landscape with natural forces interacting with the site.

and woodland, suggesting a fore-dune condition on a larger lake or ocean body. The next step is to diagram some natural forces that are likely to engage the site. Continuing with the blue pencil, diagrammatically represent these forces interacting with the site (wind, water movement, sun energy, micro-climate conditions, etc.). The example illustrates: the confluence of intense sun energy directed shoreward; breezes and cooler air moving off the water body on to shore, then deflected upwards by the woodland mass; and cool air draining out from the woodland floor and into the open shoreline space. The figure provided is not meant to direct you; rather, it simply offers an example as a jump start for your own experiment. Draw a landscape, site conditions, and natural forces for a place that interests you and captures your imagination.

Frame two

In the second frame, sketching with a blue pencil first, redraw the site, its characteristics, and its on-site natural forces. As with earlier exercises, do not concern yourself with duplicating the image in frame one when drawing it as the base for frame two. Rather, feel free to adjust and

Example of Exercise 2, frame two – imagining the natural forces interacting on the site (diagrammed in frame one) now influencing the expression of physical forms responsive to and cooperating with the forces.

modify the basic site information (illustrated in frame one) when transposing it to frame two. The purpose of the second frame is to begin the process of finding forms that interact with and are responsive to the natural forces.

Take advantage of the visual thinking and expression of interacting forces (diagrammed in frame one) to generate a physical response, a built response portrayed with imaginary forms. The example provided depicts the sun's energy, the cool air moving to the shore, and the micro-climate draining out from the woodland becoming patterns for tangible, physical elements on the site. The diagrammatic expression of the three forces suggests an imaginary ordering system that guides the making of a structure or form.

Frame two is transitional to the closing frame. It develops imagery that senses and implies possible forms by drawing them. Figuratively, by way of drawing, depictions of on-site forces and systems are married with models of structure and form.

Frame three

The third and final frame expands on the discoveries in frame two. This step illustrates a more tangible translation of the image in frame two. To heighten the discovery potential, shift to a new vantage point, and use a different drawing convention. Enrich this experiment by drawing frame three in perspective view rather than in section/elevation view

Example of Exercise 2, frame three – transposing the notions of force-generated forms in frame two to represent a designed/built landscape (changing the viewpoint used in prior frames, and illustrated in a near-eye-level perspective sketch).

(as was used in frames one and two). The example provided demonstrates advancing the experiment by viewing the landscape from offshore, illustrating the form possibilities in a near-eye-level perspective view. It visualizes a series of forms (structures) that might serve as shelters or shade structures, flanked by native vegetation masses. The structural composition in frame three derives its design cues from the patterning expressed diagrammatically in frame two.

The example provided for Exercise 2: established a shoreline site on a substantial body of water; framed the site with a mature woodland; then assumed three principal natural forces converging on and across the site. As the experiment progressed, diagrammatic representations of the three forces provided visual patterning, providing a model from which to compose structures. This drawing experiment sought and generated design ideas.

The intention of these and other form-finding exercises is not to design believable, buildable, or useful forms as final outcomes. Form-finding experiments generate possibilities for design – design ideas. They become more generous with ideas when they are temporarily freed from the responsibility to fulfill specific programmatic purposes and "functions." Formfinding experiments aid in expanding a designer's design vocabulary.

CARRY ON

After completing these two exercises, reflect on the process and the results. Refer back to the final section of Chapter 1 ("Reflections on the drawing experiments"). Consider and address the questions that were posed in that section, now relating them to the form-finding exercises. Before you move on to Chapter 3, set up and complete a couple more form-finding exercises. In a new practice round, start with different site conditions and different landforms. Choose a different set of traits, qualities, systems, and forces to deal with in the new exercises.

REFERENCES

Lappe, M. *Of All Things Most Yielding*. New York: McGraw-Hill, 1972.

McHarg, I. L. *Design with Nature* (25th anniversary edition). New York: John Wiley and Sons, 1992.

McHarg, I. L. *The Essential Ian McHarg: Writings on Design and Nature*. Ed. F. R. Steiner. Washington, DC: Island Press, 2006.

Sullivan, L. H. *The Tall Office Building Artistically Considered*. Ann Arbor: University of Michigan Library, 1922 (first published 1896).

FIELD SKETCHING TO TRANSLATION: THE ALGEBRA AND GEOMETRY OF DESIGNERS

3

Synopsis: This chapter demonstrates travel-related field sketching coupled with design experimentation. While on the road, designers can experience and draw records of inspiring landscapes and artifacts, while, in parallel, pondering and drawing design ideas based upon the space or object recorded. A comparison is provided between applied mathematics and field sketching used more broadly to generate design alternative simulations.

Field sketch – composite drawing, studying features of a vernacular rural village; drawings record various viewpoints and scales (Lanckorona, Poland).

> **Primary learning outcome:** By the end of this chapter, students will be able to generate their own visual (and captioned) archive of drawings referencing design principles they have seen, assessed, and recorded using field sketching. Included in this outcome, students will be able to formulate and draw a new, distinctive, and contemporary design idea, discovered within and transposed from the field-recorded design principles.
>
> ---
>
> **Relevance to landscape architectural students and professionals:** Landscape architects need to experience design precedents firsthand. Field sketching provides a direct and memorable record of precedents. By accumulating these records, designers generate a personal design library, a dynamic resource ready to apply in their quest to design. As the sketch records accumulate, they influence a broadened awareness of good design. Consistently recording design principles – those seen, experienced, and considered in-place – enhances the designer's ability to discern. These visual records become even more useful when used as a basis for a second step – a translation. Immediately following a sketch, a parallel process illustrates an imaginary design application, putting the original sketch to work, influencing the design of something or some place. A simple drawing that transforms observed design characteristics into a new (hypothetical) design equips designers with an enlarged capacity to generate original and novel designs. Building a personal design library is vital to fulfilling real-project work with freshness.

THE SKETCH – GROUNDWORK FOR DESIGN

Students of environmental design are trained early on to sketch, and sketch often. Drawing is a foundation for seeing, understanding, and interpreting the world. Developing the lifestyle of a designer includes regularly recording and analyzing the features and schemes that comprise the visible world. Drawing (sketching) stimulates visual thinking. It cultivates the designer's awareness about design. The act of drawing and the sketch are the designer's antennae. They generate receptivity and sensitivity to the aspects of design that are ever present, obvious, and subtle. Drawing keeps the designer attentive. They grasp characteristics of spaces, objects, systems, and processes – both natural and cultural.

Field sketch – drawing of a water feature and a sculpture in a public park, including a distant view of the Petronas Twin Towers (Kuala Lumpur, Malaysia).

Frequent sketching increases the scope and capabilities of designers. When sketching, designers engage a new way of seeing. The sketch peers into and well beyond the surface of an object or scene. Design students are consistently prodded throughout

62   FIELD SKETCHING TO TRANSLATION

sketching drills to draw what they truly see, feel, and sense. They are encouraged to guard against drawing what the mind thinks it sees, steering clear of the literal view, moving towards a valuable interpretation. Drawing carries the designer from sight to insight.

A rigorous field sketching routine, sketching what is seen and experienced while out and about, is considered the capstone for building design awareness. Journal pages can be filled with images and related text notations. They form a narrative while securing memories of a given experience, much like a storyboard for a play or film. The sketch records can describe a moment, summarize a place, script an encounter, and formulate a point of view. They can be performed to develop elaborate records of sequential experiences while moving through noteworthy environments, or they can carve out a little piece or object that may evidence a grand yet illusive whole. Reviewed later, back home, these sketches and captions become useful catalysts for design ideas. Sketches are recalled and readily accessible to stimulate and populate a full design process.

FIELD SKETCHING + DESIGN

Field sketching, from the vantage point of designers, produces keepsakes and reminders. They catch hold of an encounter, authoring a visual short story, the life and times of a space, a design. They become editorial summaries, compressing and internalizing valued points of view, seen through the lens of design. Sketches are formed using symbols and characters, visual shorthand. Lines, shapes, tones, and textures are added, subtracted, layered, divided, and multiplied, leading to a computation, a calculation, a reckoning – a sketch. The sketch becomes a visual narrative spelled out in an emblematic language. It assembles codes, sounding out the most memorable and instructive design attributes. It becomes a conclusion, a signature of a place and experience, but at the same time a springboard for new designs.

Neurological research would classify field sketching as fulfilling the preparation and background for *creativity*. Field sketching

Field sketch – composite drawing, studying landscape and greenhouse structure (Davies Alpine House, Kew Gardens, London, UK).

accumulates explicit knowledge. The sketching habit gathers up parts and portions of the whole. Granted, sketching is comprehensive, to some extent. It integrates the seeing, the thinking, and the drawing in order to express a notion of a complex whole. On this level, sketching performs aspects of synthesis. But the tools and techniques involved in sketching require the seeking of visual knowledge to be built up step-by-step, like integers interacting to produce a sum, an answer. For example, the amateur woodworker grows to master craftsman after assembling piece upon piece of explicit experience – a yearly harvest of bits of knowledge and judgments. Over time these bits fuse together into the rich operational collective – implicit knowledge. The amateur gradually transforms into the master, fully operational with a suite of implicit knowledge. The true mastery arrives as a result of continual gathering and application of the explicit knowledge over time. Woodworking, at the master's level, is attained through much practice of the working of wood. Design mastery is quite the same: it is attained through much practice of the working of design. Sketching is an important way to practice design.

Sketching is part of design training and aids in building design readiness. Indeed, routine and repetitive field sketching is acquisition

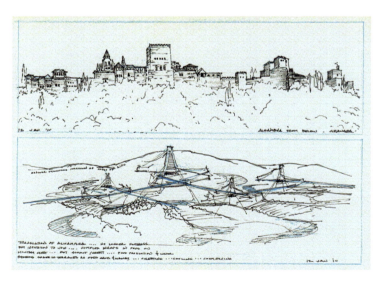

Field sketch – two-frame study, utilizing a drawing of the Alhambra (Granada, Spain) to generate a design experiment, translating a fortified city into an open and inviting futurist form, sited mid-slope rather than on the summit.

– the gathering of explicit nuggets of visual knowledge. But, intrinsically, field sketching alone does not automatically build a full breadth and scope of design knowledge, design understanding, design discernment, or design judgment. Sketching records, when used to trigger another step, a design discovery step, form bridges, linking explicit knowledge to coalesce into implicit knowledge. The sketch, therefore, establishes the next assignment, the next questions.

When completed, a sketch immediately poses a series of questions to the designer. How can the design principles gleaned from this record be applied in another context, or to another design? How can the attributes noted in the sketch be translated into design possibilities? How might the image spur relevant design ideas? Does the sketch exhibit some visual phrases or spatial language that may be useful in future designs?

MATHEMATICS, GEOMETRY, AND ALGEBRA – FIELD SKETCHING AND DESIGN DRAWING

Appreciating how field sketching can set up and promote design discoveries is illustrated in applied mathematics. The fields of geometry and algebra train students to become math practitioners – designers of answers and models, designers of knowledge. The disciplines of geometry and algebra involve rich diagnostic thinking, illustrative outcomes, and very beautiful pictures of a different sort. Those dedicated to applied mathematics participate in expeditions. They trust in the journey of mathematics, assured that exercises and sets ultimately reveal explanations. They are committed to a pioneering spirit, utilizing mathematical principles to discover answers about real-world phenomena and solutions to real-world problems.

Geometry is considered to have developed as a practice prior to algebra. It married mathematics with visualization first to express, then to explain, shapes and patterns observed in living and inert components of the world. Geometry has been trusted by mathematical practitioners and scientists since Euclid. Later, algebra developed the use of abstract symbols and arithmetic calculations first to inquire, then to consider or ponder, and finally to explain – to establish knowledge about the world decisively, illustrated in mathematical terms. Galileo often combined geometrical and algebraic modelling to articulate his findings more fully. Algebra grew to be considered even more sophisticated and nuanced than geometry in showing the way to understanding the nature of things. Algebraic equations have grown to be very commanding, directing modern physical sciences and engineering. Mathematical scientists are convinced of the benefits of their crafted equations. They are confident that these numerically expressed models describe

Field sketch – studying the prominence of sequential view-framing in Yu Garden (Old City, Shanghai, China).

attributes of the world carefully and accurately. This, they assert, is the language of the universe.

Mathematics, like design, is an experimental and exploratory field of inquiry. It is popular to describe experimental disciplines as founded on taking risks, with practitioners defined as risk-takers. This perspective misses a deeper and more fundamental point. Risk-taking can inaccurately suggest that experimentation and exploration are unplanned, or even careless or carefree. Certainly, experimentation aimed at discovering new ways, fresh answers, whether in mathematics or design, surrenders some control to the unknown, the unexpected, and the unpredictable. But experimental inquiry is not necessarily aimless, inherently dangerous, or laced with threat. Experimentation and exploration, in the context of the sciences and design, is grounded in trustworthy methods. These methods are intentional, probing imaginatively and carefully, anticipating fresh approaches and new answers. They are focused and persistent, casting out feelers and testing the waters, but with feet set firmly on the shore. They are not risk-taking ventures. They are imaginative inquiries, opening up and securing opportunities for discovery.

Similar to design thinking, algebraic thinking begins simply. The processing then grows more elaborate as sub-questions surface, eventually enabling a comprehensive mathematical question to be resolved by way of

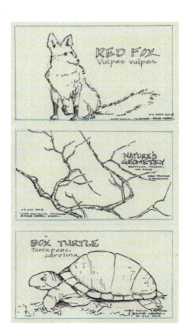

Field sketch – three-frame study of a red fox (taxidermy example), branching patterns, and a box turtle (live, in a terrarium), studying forms and geometries found in natural environments (Eagle Creek Park Earth Discovery Center, Indianapolis, USA).

advanced calculations. The initial focus is on fundamental operations and processes rather than extensive reckoning of numbers and computations. This is similar to designers beginning a design process with simple diagrams and thumbnail sketches. As algebra is studied and applied in this way, the rules for manipulating letters, numbers, and symbols in equations are not arbitrary. Instead, they are a natural extension of what is known to produce more meaningful and full-fledged computations over the long term.

Computation, like design, is fundamentally a reconciling initiative. Algebraic studies and experiments look to discover unifying principles from observable incidents and trends. Algebra is a champion at resolving numeric relationships that at first seem contradictory. Algebra constructs a harmonious solution, settling or balancing each side of an equation, resulting in a unified answer. This quite closely resembles a description of the purposes, the processes, and the results of landscape architectural design.

Mathematicians literally see numbers and numeric relationships in everything: math explains reality; reality is mined through math. "Pure mathematics is, in its way, the poetry of logical ideas. [By seeking] logical beauty spiritual formulas are discovered necessary for the deeper penetration into the laws of nature" (Einstein 1935). For many, poetry is a form of explaining phenomena, describing experiences, putting words and phrases to work to dig deep, to express the meanings of things. Poetry describes states of emotion and feelings – internal and external. When eulogizing a respected colleague – the gifted mathematician Emmy Noether – Albert Einstein described her use of mathematics as "eloquent," like a poetic language. He felt that Noether shared her mathematical insights generously. He expressed the notion that mathematics is a language that gives, uniting the contributions of an artist, an investigator, and a thinker.

Einstein, Noether, and all mathematicians trust numbers in relation to other numbers. They trust their practice and its role

FIELD SKETCHING TO TRANSLATION 69

Field sketch – composite drawing, studying features of a vernacular floating village on the Mekong River; drawings record various viewpoints and scales (Siem Reap, Cambodia).

---

in computing answers. They are certain that their practice helps explain the universe, the world, and humanity's place amidst it all. Mathematicians, just like poets and designers, are confident that they are contributing to the betterment of humanity and nature.

70 FIELD SKETCHING TO TRANSLATION

They are certain that the mathematical path to discovery results in meaningful, reasoned, logical, and ordered illustrations that serve the world with useful ideas and valuable understanding. Mathematics is

Field sketch – studying confluence of vertical forms in temple complex (Grand Palace, Bangkok, Thailand).

FIELD SKETCHING TO TRANSLATION 71

equally as expressive and meaningful as words that frame poetry, and drawings that impart design.

Much earlier, Galileo voiced similar ideas about mathematics. The following statement, translated and paraphrased, helps to illustrate an analogy between geometry and algebra, and drawing and design.

> Philosophy [nature] is written in that great book that ever lies before our eyes – I mean the universe – but we cannot understand it if we do not first learn the language and grasp the symbols [characters] in which it is written. [This book] is written in mathematical language, and the letters are triangles, circles and other geometrical figures, without which one wanders in vain through a dark labyrinth humanly unable to comprehend a single word.
>
> (Galileo Galilei quoted in Burtt 2003: 75)

Through his extensive experimental practices, Galileo convinced many that discoveries yielding enlightenment about the world are always explained by mathematical models. He held that understanding nature's systems, phenomena, and traits (visible and invisible) can and must be achieved through the precise and revealing lens of mathematics.

Most are familiar with Galileo's discoveries about falling and rolling objects with regard to their performance in motion. Galileo was committed to proving that free-falling objects and objects rolling down an inclined plane, of different materials and weights, all accelerate at an equal rate. This theory directly challenged the long-held and "logical" notion that heavier objects must fall or roll faster than lighter ones. Historical records vary as to how Galileo proved these theories and qualified them as law. It is not certain that he devised his law of freefall through hands-on experiments. Some feel that his experiments were all conducted in his mind; that he carried them out solely in an arena of mathematical thoughts. However, there is substantial evidence that he did conduct a number of hands-on experiments with objects rolling down inclined planes.

72 FIELD SKETCHING TO TRANSLATION

Nothwithstanding the questions about his methods, however, Galileo's discoveries were and remain profound and ingenious. His insights prompted a chain-reaction of inquiries leading to numerous vital discoveries in mathematics, physics, and astronomy.

Galileo was competent when explaining complicated behaviors in nature. His extensive inquiries and experimentation were eventually expressed in condensed mathematical code. His algebraic equation for characterizing a falling body is $s = 1/2at^2$. This equation is static until it is brought to life when values are inserted and a real event of motion – of falling – is portrayed, then interpreted. His mathematical methods drew him towards and led him into his very important discovery about falling bodies. The phenomenon of objects falling through space and time could be described and understood using an algebraic construct. The equation evidenced the beauty of nature, its patterns and principles. Galileo's techniques enabled him to describe an object's *fall* and also generated insight about the falling *object* itself. He beautifully illustrated motion as a system, motion as a design.

Visiting and considering Galileo's mathematical-based inquiry offers valuable instruction for designers. It is his method that warrants notice. He demonstrated a pattern of locating concepts, generating ideas, before he worked towards forming answers. He framed inquiry about the movement of objects in a step-wise fashion, over a number of years. He employed observations and records of natural phenomena to feed his thinking, his imagination. In turn, he visualized and implemented experiments that would illustrate the underlying nature of motion – revealing the design of motion. He brought forward, from the background to the foreground, ways to illustrate a fresh and lucid explanation of how objects truly act and interact with their context while moving.

In Galileo's case, he finalized his illustrations with mathematics. He used numbers and symbols in relationships that formed a balanced equation that illustrated objects, motion, and inertia in a way never seen before. In the designer's case, environments (designed and natural) are productively codified in the exercise called a *field sketch*, which then stimulates the imagination to see and draw a new idea – a design never previously envisioned.

Galileo, Einstein, Noether, and many applied mathematicians, throughout history and now, provide tool sets to investigate, record,

Field sketch – collage-style drawing integrating sketches of shells and date palm trees, inspiring a design experiment imaging a water-harvesting pavilion form, inspired by the geometries and patterns of these tropical elements (Grand Turk Island, Turks and Caicos Islands).

74 FIELD SKETCHING TO TRANSLATION

and then explain attributes about this wonderful and surprising world. Insight naturally yearns to be expressed to the benefit of all. In mathematics, the expression is achieved using a system of symbols – equations that share understanding and knowledge. The expressions solve and resolve many former unknowns. Algebra and geometry have advanced through the centuries to prove themselves invaluable at dissecting, then discovering, and finally explaining phenomena. The resultant equations describe physical relationships in a precise, internally consistent manner. They generate cohesive explanations, expressed in quantitative and qualitative terms; the attributes and actions of nature illustrate the nature of nature.

EQUATION, CONVERSION, TRANSLATION – SKETCH BEGETS DESIGN IDEA

In this parallel perspective, comparing the practice of applied mathematics to the use of field sketching to discover new design ideas, field sketching itself, does not complete or balance the equation. It is the opening of an investigation. Field sketching comes with an additional responsibility if the outcome is to be design discovery, rather than merely the sketch itself.

Field sketching naturally opens a door to practice design, to experiment with design. The sketched and captioned records display a new design lesson. Any sketch of an object, building, or space bids a designer to envision a design expression based upon principles logged in the sketch. This step-two translation or extrapolation drawing will be fresh and full of insight. Field sketches present a puzzle to diagnose, to dissect, to discover the systems, the parts, and the patterns that collectively display visual clues found in the scene. They are not passive records; they are active inquiry. They reveal the ways in which space and forms are fashioned. They codify the nature of design manifested in an object or place of interest.

While on site the sketch image grasps and exposes patterns and principles that instinctively stir up thoughts, then new observations.

These are second-tier observations; multiple interpretations arise. They are new observations found in the sketch – fresh and not altogether previously apparent by looking at and sketching the scene or object. The original sketch is the growing medium for a design experiment. It accesses understanding that naturally wants to be extended, translated, or extrapolated. It germinates an invented or designed space – a "What else could this become?" cohort. This is a form of field sketching that is curious, where the initially drawn record is understood to be only halfway there. It is now ready to ask about further and future notions, to spawn imaginative design prospects.

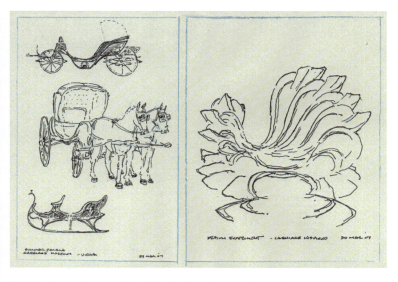

Field sketch – two-frame study, utilizing drawing of museum-housed carriages to generate a design experiment; graceful attributes of historic carriage forms expressed in an abstract ornamental image (Schönbrunn Palace, Vienna, Austria).

EXERCISE 1: GENERATING A PERSONAL DESIGN LIBRARY

Purpose of design library

It is time to sketch, then translate. It is time to complete an equation. The equation equals a sketched record of an object or space, balanced on the other side by a "So what, then?" In this exercise, ask a small and simple sketch of a view or object: "So what?" Then answer that question with a design idea that claims: "This is what it could *also* be." Maintaining a "So what?" dialog with every sketch produced affords immediate and enjoyable opportunities to envision and draw another design idea. The idea is based upon some principles revealed in the original sketch.

In this exercise, review the eight examples of field sketches and their transformation into design possibilities, design ideas. Most of the examples are small, simple, thumbnail sketches that were recorded during study tours abroad. They were developed to seek out a global appreciation for the principles of design – ancient and contemporary. It is important to appreciate that these field-based drawing exercises do not have to be achieved on a grand tour or during exotic travel experiences. There are many design principles to find and observe locally, simply by leaving your studio desk, workplace, or home and heading outside for a stroll-and-sketching session. The field trip aspect is far from essential. If participating in a field study program while reading this chapter, perform these design library exercises by sketching subjects that are in your daily path of travel. If not, simply find objects and spaces that interest and engage your design sensibilities in your local surroundings. The benefits of developing a design library are numerous, regardless of where the sketches are made.

A simple form of this experimentation involves side-by-side drawings. One side is the first-hand sketch of an object or space; the other is its translation into a different application. Recall that experimentation does not always require strict adherence to a project-specific application. These experiments have great value in the realm of thought-building (design thinking) in union with skill-building.

Exercise 1 accomplishes a wide variety of bite-size seek-and-find design experiments. As the examples illustrate, a design library accumulates over a period of time, based on multiple field sketching outings. As with all previous exercises, these thumbnail – or vignette – experiments should be quick, immediate, and expressive. They should not be too detailed and not painstakingly performed. The base sketch and short caption (left side) and its inspired translation and short descriptive caption (right side) together provide a small taste of design. Each side-by-side experiment provides a moment to analyze while sketching a scene, then immediately provides an opportunity to sketch a fresh and new design idea. Together, they provide a moment to practice designing.

The field sketching – triggering a design translation – provides a quick yet structured opportunity to dissect and expose the inner systems, driving forces, and notable characteristics within a scene, environment, or object. The simple thumbnail sketch or record (left side) exposes and notes significant natural and cultural components that capture design principles. The principles are there in the sketch (left side). They are evidenced in observable objects, artifacts, built environments, as well as cultural customs that are found in a place, now coded in the sketch.

Then the translation (right side) immediately draws an impression. It extracts a principle, a force, a form language, or a geometric system and invents a diagrammatic image that suggests a possible application. The translation is an unjudged image of a designed place, space, structure, or object – at no specific scale and in no particular site or geographic context.

Instructions for developing a design library

Utilize the following examples only as a jump start for developing a personalized design library. Start the various pages using a large sketchbook (e.g. 21 × 30 cm; 8.5 × 11.8 in). Notice the topics for each full page:

1. Design and planning principles.
2. Ordering systems, organizational patterns, and form languages.
3. The "heart" and the "art."
4. Detailing characteristics.

Completed page of a design library, emphasizing *design and planning principles* that have been recorded, then translated to alternative design ideas.

Below:
Design and planning principles – one enlarged example.

With a non-photo blue pencil, first set up each page with a simple matrix and framework (square images, approximately 3.5 × 3.5 cm; 1.5 × 1.5 in). Also with the blue pencil, prepare the page with lettering guidelines beside each image frame, as shown in the examples.

Again, utilize the examples only as aids to launch yourself on a personal quest to develop a design library. Remember, generating a design library is for the purpose of enjoying moments of experimental design. Each pair is a simple practice of design. Engage briefly in the spark that connects design thinking

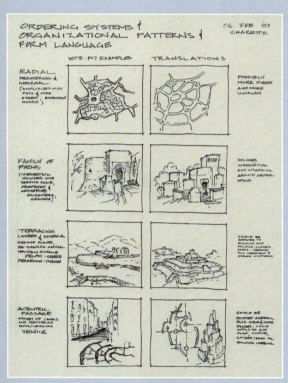

Completed page of a design library, emphasizing *ordering systems* that have been recorded, then translated to alternative design ideas.

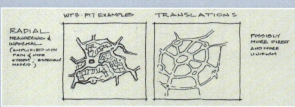

Below: Ordering systems – one enlarged example.

to a transformation, to a design outcome – a simple, little drawing. Enjoy the quick and refreshing arc between an observation (sketch) and the immediate conversion to an alternative application (translation). Delight in this private and personal practice of the design process. It is a productive and rewarding step, expanding one's capabilities as a fresh and insightful designer.

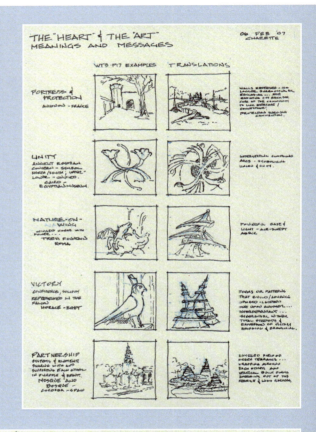

Completed page of a design library, emphasizing *the "heart" and the "art"* that has been recorded, then translated to alternative design ideas.

The "heart" and the "art" – one enlarged example.

Anticipate that these expanded field sketching methods, followed by translations, will fuel freshness in a wide range of design inquiries. Expect these design library sketching activities to advance design problem-solving as they generate many surprising and helpful design ideas.

Completed page of a design library, emphasizing *design detailing* that has been recorded, then translated to alternative design ideas.

Design detailing – one enlarged example.

EXERCISE 2: EXPANDED DESIGN TRANSLATIONS

The techniques that were employed in Exercise 1 are also utilized in this exercise. But here the drawings are larger than thumbnails. These sketches look more closely at a design or planning principle evidenced in day-to-day life and the environment around us.

In Exercise 2 the act of discovering (translating) a design idea is based upon an initial field sketch of a landscape scene, a built structure, and/or natural or designed objects. The initial sketch is more detailed than those in Exercise 1.

As with previous exercises, once the field sketch is completed, immediately proceed through one or two additional steps. The characteristics recorded and analyzed in the original sketch drive the development of the next drawing – a translation, a design experiment.

A large sketchbook page (e.g. 21 × 30 cm; 8.5 × 11.8 in) is ideal for these more detailed and zoomed-in design experiments. The examples demonstrate either a two-frame or a three-frame set-up.

The initial field sketch is still the foundation, the key to finding new ideas. The sketching process dissects and exposes principles, systems, driving forces, and notable characteristics within the scene or object. This analysis-while-drawing triggers thoughts and visual images that can be transferred to a fresh and original application.

Then, as the examples illustrate, the experiment moves into new territory – new ideas. Draw an expression, an impression, a translation in the next frame. The experimental drawing extracts a principle, a force, a form language, or a geometric system and invents a new image, visualizing an entirely different application. As before, free the translation from any form of judgment – simply lay it down, draw loosely, as you think about a new way of looking at characteristics recorded in the field sketch.

Two-step translation – a landscape sketch of ancient burial sites inspires a form study, imagining a landform and building complex (Valley of the Kings, Luxor, Egypt).

Exercise 2 presents opportunities to practice design with a higher resolution of outcome. It affords drawing at a more resolved scale, resulting in more detailed design expressions. Utilize the examples to stimulate and launch your own enjoyable personal studies. Anticipate the discovery of original design ideas from these experimental drawing techniques.

Two-step translation – a collage-like sketch, including features typical of a semi-arid landscape in western USA (e.g. granite boulders, coniferous trees and bark, pine cones, pine needles, etc.), inspires an image of a gateway or trailhead in a natural park, drawing from patterns and geometries of native materials (near Lake Tahoe, Nevada, USA).

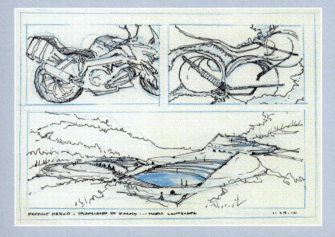

Three-step translation – a highly designed contemporary motorcycle sketch inspires a form study in step two; then the form study is translated into an imaginary park complex in step three.

REFERENCES

Burtt, E. A. *The Metaphysical Foundations of Modern Science*. Mineola, NY: Dover Publications, 2003 (first published 1924).

Einstein, A. The Late Emmy Noether: Professor Einstein Writes in Appreciation of a Fellow-Mathematician. *New York Times*, May 4, 1935: 12.

Sharratt, M. *Galileo: Decisive Innovator*. Cambridge: Cambridge University Press, 1994.

INNER PRECEDENTS: DESIGN IDEAS DRAWN FROM VIGILANT OBSERVATION

4

Review: The earlier chapters established the grounds for becoming more fluent and more broadly based as designers – good and refreshing designs do not just happen. Regularly setting up and fulfilling graphic-thinking exercises, images representing design ideas, is the sharpening stone of design as craft. Practicing design is just as critical to the fitness of design professionals as sports practice is to athletes who aspire to achieve Olympic medals. Practice produces design preparedness, design readiness.

INNER PRECEDENTS

Synopsis: This chapter presents theories about observation-based learning, and their usefulness in fostering design explorations of a more complex and holistic nature. The social and behavioral science theories presented are shown to drive exploratory design from different points of view. The narrative and chapter-end exercises guide students to discover clues that inform design possibilities relevant to site-design projects. The explorations outlined in this chapter augment traditional design methods. The drawing-based explorations tap into imaginative design possibilities. Without these exploratory exercises, valuable design ideas could go undiscovered in project work that demands fast-turnaround conclusions. These visually communicated explorations are likened to one's own design precedents, from which one discerns new and enriching design directions. Self-generated or imagined precedents interact with one's design thinking, generating fruitful ideas for innovative design application.

Field sketch – design exploration, imagined serpentine environmental art, sinuous façade amendments, and meandering ground-plane patterns interlaced within existing orthogonal order.

Primary learning outcome(s): By the end of this chapter, students will be able to generate a variety of their own site-design explorations, driven by clues gleaned from site characteristics, from site performance criteria, and from rudimentary design-program requirements. The clues spur design possibilities drawn from site features (ecological, contextual, and structural characteristics).

Students will also understand how to utilize design performance expectations in order to nurture form possibilities. They will have performed a variety of gymnastic-like drawing explorations that express form, patterns, and site-planning ordering systems that help uncover site-design possibilities. As a result, they will generate intriguing form ideas that heighten the aesthetic values in their personal project work. These explorations increase the designers' confidence. Students will experience a boost to their originality, allowing them to apply unique artistry within their design process, design outcomes, and design presentations.

Relevance to landscape architectural students and professionals: Designers are recognized as individuals who are trained to convey innovation in the design and construction of sites, places, and space. A thorough and full-spectrum design process requires that experimental and extemporaneous contributors regularly engage with and augment the pragmatic and technical performance requirements for good design. The exercises in this chapter provide quick paths to imaginative, fresh, and artistic ideas. The exercise results readily enlighten design work and are helpful in fulfilling demands for swift and thorough design solutions formed with artistry.

DESIGN KEENNESS: OBSERVING AND LEARNING FROM A SKETCH

Originality is a key responsibility for designers. Being fully equipped to design – being design ready – is being conditioned to formulate original ideas. Cultivating individuality or uniqueness as a designer involves frequent self-structured learning initiatives. Self-learning is truly rewarding – it fosters outlooks and views that are distinct to the individual. Facilitating one's own education provides unique circumstances within which to learn. Self-learning is personalized and therefore fun. It carries with it the joy of generating one's own tests, quizzes, and experiments.

Self-learning can be understood as practicing, but it is value-added practice intent on expanding and growing more skills and new insights. For designers, self-learning is an inventive form of practice.

88   INNER PRECEDENTS

It goes beyond maintaining skills at current levels. Practicing design – by processing, generating, and illustrating design ideas – expands the skills range. It increases one's agility in processing designs, broadening the reach and scope of design thinking. This is design readiness.

This self-learning does not demand self-teaching. It means arranging and structuring exercises that heighten one's sensitivity It is a form of design-learning enriched by acute observations, by keen examinations – expecting surprises. Practicing, in the form of design exercises, lays out a field for learning. Presenting onese f with a sketch of visual information (e.g. patterns, forms, lines, and shapes) ignites a design-thinking sequence. The sketch begins a process; it *is* a process. The sketch plays with and prods one's design mind.

The act of drawing is accompanied simultaneously by multiple observations. A design exercise, a sketch, builds a laboratory calling for sharp and prompt observations. These observations then rapidly generate thoughts and statements – a seminar of self-learning. While drawing, the designer is pulled into an inner conversation with the ever-changing image. The conversation is between what is in the image now and what will – or should – be next. This dialog is invigorating. It issues in a chain reaction, fueling more observations, married with questions. As observations are processed, turned over and under, they naturally lead the conversation to questions – a quiz that stimulates insight and inspiration. Inventive design explorations empower self-learning. They transform, they inform, they advise design and designers.

Key to this essential observation-based connection is carefully directed surveillance and reflection. It also needs spontaneity and quickness so as not to overthink. Drawing something – *anything* – is one means of producing an opportunity to observe. Drawing-generated observation is characterized by active and direct engagement. It motivates alert and intent peering. It provokes rapt and attentive thought.

INNER PRECEDENTS 89

Field sketch – studying the *Cloud Gate* sculpture, set amidst towering forms and clouds overhead (Millennium Park, Chicago, USA).

90 INNER PRECEDENTS

Action-oriented observations are accompanied by the designer believing to enter a fruitful conversation while drawing, while designing. These conversations are most pure and intimate when they flow eagerly through hand-drawn dialog. When drawing is the venue, the visually based observations and conversations do not form passive records. Rather, they perform valuable discourse, exchange, a concert of design possibilities. This is a form of drawing that stirs up collaboration, bridging design possibilities (what could be) with design forms welcomed by a site. Experimental drawing deliberately produces occasions to observe and consider, heightening a designer's awareness. It teaches lessons on how sites invite imaginative design possibilities – promising, vivid, and insightful design ideas.

The term *site* in this discussion transcends well beyond a parcel of land, or a particular negative space in an urban context. This notion of site grasps and connects with the many elements and systems

Design exploration – investigating spatial means to achieve an enriched wildlife habitat for a proposed row-home cluster; form, massing, and layout study based upon flight patterns and airspace needs of urban bird species (raptors, finches, songbirds, etc.).

that interdependently operate in a place. A considerate way to employ the term *site* is to appreciate that designs, when finally implemented and built, are best when the design has emerged as a respectful answer to the site's invitation to host an intervention (an intercession). Graceful guests reflect the grace of the host. The array of elements comprising a site includes a community of physical attributes and dynamic forms. It contains active and passive natural systems at all heights, breadths, and depths. A site incorporates the diverse interlaced and expectant place-players and users, like animals, vegetables, and minerals. And, of course, a site includes the people – the sanctioned human partners. Employing a science-based vocabulary, a site includes multi-tiered operating systems. It hosts intermingling and interacting systems, including eco-systems, social systems, economic systems, and aesthetic systems. These systems are interdependent and interoperational – ready, willing, and able to partner in fresh ways with watchfully designed elements.

SCIENCE OF OBSERVATIONAL LEARNING

Landscape architects design environments that deliver experiences. The experiences unfold largely in the visual domain. Becoming well prepared to design necessitates learning to see more deeply, more carefully. The designer's vow is to enact a design process that is watchful, sympathetic, and conscious. This vigilance is achieved with observation, attentive to what surrounds the mission to design, more than focusing on the design itself. This vow diminishes tendencies to design-by-opinion, favoring design-by-facilitation. Honoring a site in a design process necessitates sensing and seeing the many and varied elements and systems that operate within a site.

Observation-based design experiments engage comprehensive sets of variables. They entail explorations more closely associated with real projects and real site applications. Generating design ideas using drawing-based discovery methods is closely associated with principles and theories found in behavioral and social-science disciplines. These disciplines reveal the dynamics operating in a learning experience. They illustrate how learning transforms to communicate what is

92 INNER PRECEDENTS

learned. They explain why and how observations made when drawing lead to finding valuable design ideas.

The psychologist Albert Bandura is widely cited and lauded for his theory of *observational learning*. His principles are applied to social and cultural learning, for individuals and communities. From Bandura's perspective, *observational learning* results from observing the behavior of others, which he calls models. Models are those in authority or of higher status, including an individual's parents, grandparents, older siblings, teachers, co-workers, and even similar-aged classmates or friends who are respected ard influential.

Observational learning prevails in families, communities, and entire cultures where youth are included in and even expected to perform the day-to-day activities and tasks of getting life accomplished – and therefore learn by observation *who* they are and *what* they shall become.

Bandura (1977) identifies four distinct stages of observational learning:

1. Attention. This stage involves attentiveness to what is happening around the learner. In the social/behavioral emphasis of Bandura's scholarship, this refers to close attention to the model (the influential example). The depth and extent of learning are highly dependent on what the observer expects of and looks for within the model. An engaged observer generates anticipation for learning. Active observation awakens emotions that form deeper connections – relationships – with the model. This enhances what the observer can acquire and absorb directly from the model by means of formative lessons.
2. Retention and memory. This stage acknowledges the need to remember and recall what was learned from the model in order to perform the behavior in the future. Observer–learners develop the ability to cipher this information into readi y retrievable forms. This coding is frequently established by repeating and rehearsing – practicing the newly observed behavior or trait.

3. Initiation and motor. In the third stage, observers achieve the physical and intellectual capacity to produce the observed act(s). In many cases the observer possesses the necessary responses, but reproducing the model's actions may involve skills the observer has not yet acquired. For instance, Bandura suggests that an observer may watch a juggler carefully, but mere observation will not enable the observer to juggle.
4. Motivation. In this final stage, Bandura notes a critical distinction between learning and performance. If a learner is not inspired or motivated to produce an observation-learned behavior, they will not perform it. Unless motivated, a person will not "produce" as a result of their learning. Motivation, whether from others' encouragement or from self-generated determination, is therefore key to benefiting tangibly from learning.

Design exploration – imagining interpretive center and overlook facility in canyon landscape, modeled from existing crevice formations.

94   INNER PRECEDENTS

Sites are models. They are great communicators. Designers listen and learn the site language, the site's expressions. The site and the designer commune equally in their search for *the* design. Site-guided design explorations unearth the considerations, the desires, and the prerequisites that are concurrently site spoken and designer observed. The design possibilities generated are respectful responses, attentive to the fruitful conversation. With practice, designers peer into and around sites, then detect, discern, and learn – grasping cogent comments, indeed rich and rewarding messages, from the site. Returning to the social-science perspective, the hallmarks of a constructive conversation are achieving understanding, forming insights and food for ongoing thought, and apprehending possibilities for further action. The participants grow and expand as individuals, while the community realizes mutual bounties from the exchange. All involved are better than they were before the discourse began.

Observational learning, in the realm of design exploration, is observation with conversation. It is fulfilled by carefully looking for and seeing the site, especially the arrangement of resources dwelling there. The observer–learner–designer ensures a no-fog view and open conversation by excluding preconceived notions or predetermined conclusions from the dialog. All the while, the designer brings to the exchange essential knowledge and awareness about the nature of the site. Astute observations are achieved when the designer has already accumulated a foundation in the natural and social sciences, a familiarity with the community of systems that frame the site's make-up. Designer as informed listener is vital, establishing a posture that is reciprocal, mutual believing. The designer expects the process of drawing to open a conversation with the site. The designer and drawing invite the site to respond by telling a story of design from the site's viewpoint. Responsive and ready ideas are stimulated by evidence provided by the site – from its experienced and seasoned nature. Design ideas emerge from educated discussions with the land – the site provides counsel. *The site is the model.*

Observational learning looks to discover evidence. The observational learner positions for direct and clear views. The learning, the finding of evidence, needs connection with the model, the site. It can afford no separation, no obstructions. Overcoming tendencies to approach design through habitual or superficial studies requires concerted effort. It involves casting off preconceptions. It means putting on pause other rules for thinking and maxims for acquiring knowledge. It necessitates temporarily suspending routine methods of inquiry and decision-making – those that engage automatically and unconsciously.

A clear observation–conversation interchange allows the site to signal its intricacies, revealing markers, clues, cues, and suggestions that frame the bases for distinctive design ideas. The design explorations then undertake the privilege of visually scribing the persuasive score of the conversation – articulating a fresh and coherent design tale, offered graciously, and mostly, by the site.

Design exploration – space-efficient and energy-conserving town form imagined for peninsula landform; residents dwelling in ziggurat forms wrapped in earthen terraces for high-yield food production.

96 INNER PRECEDENTS

Bandura (1977) maintains that observation leading to learning and valid insight is grasped and made operational as the learner encodes or catalogs the insight. A learner-made depository ensures thoughts and ideas are formed and packaged for recall and reuse. The recording and storing stimulate mental closure and arrange access to memory. Relating this to the design ideation analogy, the site-inspired sketch or diagram is recording, both on paper and in the mind, a design application for future recall. A design exploration generated from unbound observation is a reservoir for ideas, a cache of significant and useful insight.

EXTENSIONS – TOOLS FOR THE MINING OF IDEAS

Design is a process, a learnable process. Conveying how to design involves a wide array of teaching methods. Some instruction on how to design is fulfilled within the traditional model – teacher mentoring student. In many disciplines, either one-to-one or in a group setting, a teacher–student model draws the student along, demonstrating a means to an end. Learning is often accomplished by imitation. This is a proven and normalized cultural scheme. It is a tooled-up arrangement for teaching and learning that is familiar in most cultures. The teacher–learner mode presents how to think, how to do, how to confirm, and often how to conform. This model is very effective and appropriate in cases where the learning and the outcomes need to be linear, repeatable, and consistent.

In design education, much of the teaching and learning is shaped differently. Methods for teaching design are amended to include more diverse modes of delivery. Frequently, a teacher or mentor, called the *model* in the previous discussion (meaning the site as teacher), poses questions that spark the designer–learner to set their own course – self-motivated inquiry. The making and use of ideas, including design ideas, is what a cultural anthropologist would categorize as a modern tool – an *extension*.

A working definition for *extension* includes two interrelated concepts. An extension achieves *expansion*. It acts to expand the size, scope, and range of an application or process, increasing effectiveness in fulfilling a task or operation. An extension also achieves *addition*. It may include elements that add or are pulled out, even lengthened, increasing the reach and capacity to achieve a task. From an anthropological perspective, examples of extensions are diverse. Some are tangible, like a wheel or an axe. Others are less tangible, such as cultural values, ethical standards, and behavioral norms. Ultimately, extensions are said to promote advancements. They promote beneficial adaptations that are external to the individual, group, or society. An extension increases capabilities that may not otherwise be realized by genetic adaptation.

Although not known as a designer or an artist, and not specifically addressing design, Edward T. Hall, an anthropologist, provides valuable insight into what designers do, how they do it, and what keeps their doing pure and productive. Throughout his career as a scholar, writer, and teacher of anthropology, Hall was fascinated with people and how they aggregate into and operate as cultures. He is credited with peering in more deeply and through more layers to discover the glue, the binder, of cultures and societies. He observed and assessed the behavioral, attitudinal, and aspirational structures (both tangible and intangible) that are the true form-givers and pattern-makers of any particular culture.

Design ideas are examples of what Hall describes as *tools*, which he in turn classifies as *extensions*. In past and present cultures, observations and concepts expressed in any combination of visual symbols, words, and phrases are tools. They extend human reach and effectiveness in achieving necessary outcomes, like meaningful communication. Design drawings, as extensions, form a language, igniting a dialog with the designer. They reach out to converse; they expand, broadening forms of visual dialog, visual exchange.

In their own way, drawings speak. They talk and pose questions. Experimental drawings converse easily. Their visual discussions are plain and unassuming. They offer inquiry. They invite opportunities

98 INNER PRECEDENTS

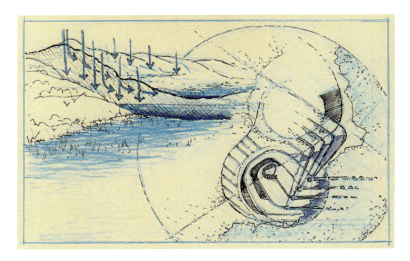

Design exploration – concept for wetland nature preserve, nature education center, and boardwalk circulation inspired by diagrammatic cross-section illustrating precipitation, infiltration, subsurface interflow, and lateral ground-water movement supplying water to the wetland basin.

---

to peer in and observe possibilities, potential routes to a design. Their questioning is friendly, non-confrontational. The process of answering is not pressured or forced. Design ideas have a tongue; they voice a unique language. The design expression stretches out, fashioning forms and functions – optional, not mandatory. These drawing extensions, like other tangible tools, endeavor to gather and fuse parts into whole systems, responding to the landscape as an intricate composite – the inert, the biotic, and the beautiful.

A unique relationship is formed between the designer and their drawing, their extension. They both participate in the discussion. The process is not a one-way-street. The designer is, in a sense, conferring with the drawing as it evolves. Throughout the exchange and interplay, the designer is the scribe, continually summarizing moments in the dialog, employing graphic symbols and forms. A drawing is built. Patterns, suggestions of environments and landscapes, materialize from two directions. It is a meeting between the person who is drawing and the drawing itself as it takes its shape, becoming external and visible.

Another way to view this dual process – the person who is drawing and the drawing coming to life – is to regard the two realms as performers. Both are acting alternately in a give-and-take presentation. The two players counsel and feed each other in a team-generated improvisation. A design idea is evidenced in the drawing. The idea is a tool, shaped and fashioned, an extension. As the players conclude the performance, the drawing is finished, design possibilities have been portrayed, a design tool has appeared.

Externalizing a design conversation by talking it out in a sketch increases the capture, the harvesting of ideas. It excites opportunities to observe. Upon observing what has appeared in an exploratory drawing, the designer is stirred to ponder. The drawing has expanded the reach of the designer's imagination, and added previously unrealized possibilities.

> Extensions often permit man to solve problems in satisfactory ways, to evolve and adapt at great speed without changing the basic structure of his body. However, the extension does something else: it permits man to examine and perfect what is inside the head. Once something is externalized, it is possible to look at it, study it, change it, perfect it, and at the same time learn more important things about oneself. The full implications of the extension as lessons and the extension as mirror have yet to be fully realized.
>
> (Hall 1976: 29)

Hall enlarges the concept of extensions from the anthropological perspective. He notes that extensions often provide alternate or even skewed perches from which to see and understand aspects of life from a different angle and unique point of view. Design exercises provide these perches or platforms for design projects. A design

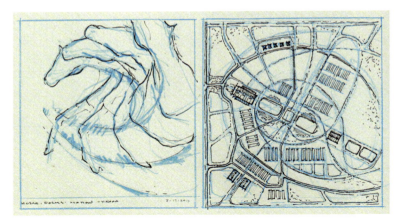

Design exploration – overlaid time-lapse sketches of horses galloping and rearing stimulates masterplan study for equestrian competition facility.

exploration begins as flashes and sparks, deep internal notions, then it flows, readily exported to its external tangible form – a drawing. The drawing grabs and charts the evidence, the flare of inspiration, the fabric of key thoughts and ideas. Though in no way a resolved design, the design exploration gains permanence. It is accessible; it may be handled, squeezed, studied, flipped over, turned upside down, and manipulated in ways that are unavailable inside the mind itself.

THE CATCH, THE CONCERN, THE TRAP – EXTENSION TRANSFERENCE

The positive attributes of an extension are its power to expand scope and effectiveness, and its ability to add capacity in achieving desired outcomes. Hall establishes that an individual's world view is shaped in an unconscious matrix of cultural patterns. These patterns are extensions; they are tools that help societies operate smoothly. But at the same time, these patterns and principles may also press for adherence and conformity. Individuals can become harnessed by these culturally set patterns to the extent that they do not really see what they are seeing. They are not really doing what they need to be doing. They are observing others' reactions; others' responses; others' behaviours; others' ways of relating to and dealing with what is there. In other words, they are no longer seeing from *within*; their seeing has become externalized, indirect, separated from themselves. They are unconsciously seeing through cultural filters, culturally limiting tools. This raises issues and concerns.

Hall notes that contemporary culture has had much experience and professed "success" in establishing less tangible extensions. It is rather standard procedure to manipulate behaviors, relationships, surroundings, and environments externally. Individuals and groups often unknowingly operationalize these external responses and practices. Over time cultural practices, processes, ideas, and mores, originally intended to guide from within, become external operators, subconscious and regimental. Hall is credited with identifying the extent to which the externalized approach takes over and operates on its own. The tool is thus in control. The operation of the tool has been transferred to the tool. The overriding force and power of the tool has been transferred from the operator to the tool itself – the oversight of the extension has been transferred.

Hall developed this caution regarding the unintentional handing over of control to extensions. He is credited with coining the anthropological construct known as *extension transference* (ET). This is the symbolic subdivision of a particular goal or purpose so that the subdivided concept seems fragmented from – or no longer related to – the original purpose.

Hall concedes that forming and institutionalizing extensions is a trend that is found in all developing and contemporary societies. But when it shifts to ET, he warns that extensions are transported to a thoughtless realm, enabling them to take on a function and permanence of their own. ET effectively results in the tool, the rule, the pattern or framework of meaning beginning to operate on its own. The extension becomes independent of the individuals and

102 INNER PRECEDENTS

Design exploration – native calligraphic form generates design ideas, illustrating infill massing and land-use configurations for a sports stadium repurposed to become a city-edge new town center.

collective who formed it in the first place. The extension can even disengage from the purposes for which it originated. The extension turns against – performs counter to – its original guiding light.

EXTENSIONS AND DESIGN IDEAS

Drawings are extensions. Drawings generate design ideas. Design ideas are extensions. Design ideas are thoughts, notions, viewpoints, impressions, and dreams – even beliefs. Design ideas listen while they also foster dialog with the site. They facilitate the making of designs molded with stewardship, imparting delight. They are the imaginative models and patterns, recommending how designs may best behave. Design ideas are tools formed to find and mire good designs. They cultivate and energize movement and direction toward a lively design result. Ideas are not the design itself, but they prepare the glue, the framework, and the vitality for inspired designs.

The concern – or "the trap" to use Hall's phrase – posed by extension transference confronts designers and design education. There is a need to stand guard. Designers and designs are subject to a form of extension transference. Traditional design solutions can become drivers, inadvertently quieting, stunting, or dulling a design's full potential. Pre-engineered solutions and templates can control design outcomes. There is an ever-present risk that what has been done before takes over. In this scenario, designing – once personal and originating from the designer – is transferred to a set of rules that now claims control. This transfer promptly supresses and clouds opportunities for innovation.

Resisting transference – the loss of oversight of design – requires holding the discovery processes close, internal, and personal. As design ideas move forward to resolve designs, the design should evidence a path that is clear, simple, and direct. Distinctive designs are nurtured, like the gardener with a hoe tending his borders. The conclusion of a personalized design process will be a design that is bright and first-hand.

The realm of design is vulnerable to extension transference. The means to establishing a design outcome can become driven by professionally and culturally ordered ways, predetermined expectations and mandates. The methods for achieving a design can be unintentionally externalized, then empowered. A design process, if reassigned to external directives, can become separated from the home of the design – the site – the provider, the host, and the source of good and responsive designs. The so-called "state-of-the-art" can hijack and stifle design innovation. Designs are not true, full, or pure if they are regulated by traditions, subjugated by standardized criteria, or subdued by compulsory expectations. The enjoyment, simplicity, and directness of designer, sketchbook, pens, and pencils engaged in candid observations and conversations with the site endure as a gentle and pleasant guard against extension transference in the realm of design.

104 INNER PRECEDENTS

Design exploration – imagining terraced landscape formed and organized to host aquaponics and intense specialty agriculture.

DESIGN EXPLORATIONS AS INNER PRECEDENTS

Design precedents often contribute powerful and compelling directions to jump-start design ideas, especially when confronted with generating landscape designs that address complex projects. Design precedents that are functioning built-works reveal others' design resolutions to similar or related project types. They can be helpful, to a point, when a new project is charged with similar design prospects, challenges, and constraints. Within design professions, precedents are often requisite start-up or datum points from which a new project should proceed. Indeed, precedents are essential models, paradigms, and exemplars to offer some bases from which to progress and to build upon. The notion that precedents are the lead-off ideas and set design requirements should be carefully considered. Precedents in the form of already-built examples should not restrict or confine the development of other types of guides and models.

By practicing design and becoming more facile in generating design ideas, self-generated precedents, or inner precedents can be born through exploration and discovery. This use of the term *precedent* (inner precedent) takes some liberties with its typical definition, implying an example that has been validated and thereby has established principles or standards. Design explorations as inner precedents are not charged with becoming case studies or exemplars. They freely investigate and look to invent, advance possibilities for moving a project forward.

Precedents that are tangible, built, and tested over time are invaluable as gauges and guides for new designs. The value of inner precedents is different. Imaginary examples of designed places or spaces provide benchmarks for new ideas from an original perspective. They are purposely unproven. They are exploratory, probing uncharted possibilities. They spark from an instance, from a point of contact with information and evidences that are self-generated in order to jump-start a unique path of design discovery. The most profitable design explorations take place as

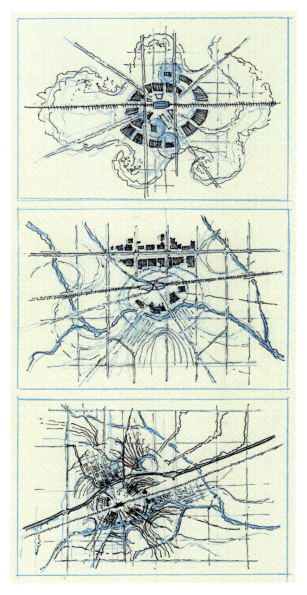

Design exploration – three-step study of city-edge transit-oriented development (TOD) node, including: diagram of mixed-use building massing for optimum pedestrian penetration to station center; future TOD infill community core in relation to exiting historic town form; and district view of TOD community contexts reorganized to accommodate intense local food production close to the community residents.

drawing events while at the project site and surroundings. For landscape architects, design ideas that best fit the project are usually uncovered on site. The site is the host for the design. It is close at hand, trustworthy, and poised to inspire.

Explorations generate possible directions for a project. They are drawing events that provide encounters, intercepting design possibilities. They are tools that amplify observations and promote intimate inquiry. A successful exploration is unjudged and unpredicted. It generates a simple possibility, a precursor to a design project. The exploration does not establish firm standards from which to base the project work, but it does provide a freshness of approach, the perch and the vantage point to find a breakthrough.

MAKING DESIGN TOOLS – PRINCIPLES, EXERCISES, AND EXAMPLES – DESIGN EXPLORATIONS

The following design explorations are provided to guide the reader in developing personal variations. As with all previous exercises and experiments, this genre of design exploration is intended to be enjoyable, to yield many surprises, and to expand one's design thinking capacities. Once again, the exercises offer opportunities to practice the act of design. They demonstrate direct and simple probing into a site's characteristics, its traits, and its visible and invisible clues. They anticipate the discovery of valuable principles that will enhance a design task. They are achieved by peering deep and beyond the surface of a site and a design assigned to transform it. The explorations – the discoveries – are represented in simple drawings, generating design possibilities that respond to forces, systems, and spatial schemes.

Enjoy setting up these exercises. They build a design toolyard. These design explorations are well suited to addressing current design assignments and project work. The earlier exercises and experiments have been structured. They have been presented prescriptively and with direct coaching. They have been framed with step-by-step instructions. By contrast, these exercises are purposely

108 INNER PRECEDENTS

less structured, encouraging individual modifications to address one's own design work.

Exploratory design drawings warrant the use a large sketchbook (e.g. 21 × 30 cm; 8.5 × 11.8 in), or similar-sized art-paper sheets of medium-valued neutral background (ivory, tan, buff, etc.).

Each of the following exercises has at its core important considerations and choices. Understanding and utilizing these considerations will aid in carrying out personalized design explorations.

A few keys to enjoyable and productive design discovery opportunities, like those demonstrated here, include:

1. Expect the drawing, the design exploration, to produce inspiration. Be confident that original design ideas will emerge.
2. Begin design explorations by observing and drawing elements of personal interest, such as attributes of a landscape, a particular site, or elements (objects) that are native to a project site.
3. Draw with enthusiasm and acute vision. Recall that these exercises do not require "art" and they are not for the making of "art." Consider a design exploration as extending one's vision with pencil, pen, and paper.
4. Drawing is an extension, a tool – an observational tool and a crafting tool. Observe through the lens of the drawing or diagram, confident it will stimulate insight. Use drawing as a tool to invent design tools, extending reach and grasp into the manifold realms of design – the immense design of things, great and small.
5. The ingredients for a rewarding design exploration include setting up a retreat. If possible, leave the workplace and head out to the project site. Get away and explore on your personal time. If traveling to the project site is unfeasible, find a private space, surrounded with photos, sketches, and items gathered

from the site. Any content related to the design project and site can inspire useful design ideas.

Design explorations, such as these, contribute to staying sharp as a designer–spokesperson for resources and systems comprising the host site and its surroundings in real project work.

EXERCISE 1: WORD-GAMING – EMOTIONAL QUALITIES STIMULATE DESIGN IDEAS

The following two examples of a design exploration utilize narrative springboards. Qualitative words or expressions are employed to trigger spatial design possibilities. This exploration technique can be thought of as word-gaming to find design ideas. In each of these examples, the base diagram (left side) is a conceptual diagram generated during client meetings at the very beginning of the project. The base diagrams show proposed building footprints and other features. The early concepts in the base diagrams set out very traditional land-use arrangements for both projects.

The next steps are the design explorations. In each example, there are three explorations (left to right), performed in sequence after the base diagram. Each exploration is set up initially by selecting qualitative words to stimulate alternative design ideas. Typically, the qualitative words have some practical significance to the purposes of the project, but the words should not be too limiting or sober since design explorations are intended to produce surprising design ideas. The words can be self-selected; they can be gathered from others who are familiar with the project and the qualities the project is expected to deliver; or they can be more spontaneously discovered (e.g. by leafing through a thesaurus). The chosen words become the driving forces for the sequence of diagrammatic studies.

Each exploration seeks to express, in visual form, the narrative qualities and sensations gleaned from the words. The purpose of the three follow-up explorations is to generate a number of optional spatial configurations for the project. The explorations discover expressive alternatives for the proposed project, deriving spatial layouts that are enhanced well beyond those initially given.

Example 1

In Example 1 the base drawing shows an urban-infill concept, including a streetside open space (plaza), surrounded by two tiers of mixed-use buildings, and a number of pedestrian passages between and around the buildings.

In this example, after setting the base (given) diagram, the exercise prepares for three successive explorations by first selecting and assigning qualitative words to work with in each of the three explorations. The first exploration selected "re-order and reflect." The second was influenced by "intensify and focus." The third derived design stimulus from "drift and float."

The explorations illustrate new design ideas for the project, noting energetic spatial configurations and enriched pedestrian movement systems.

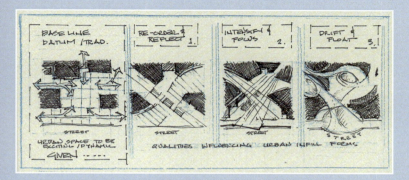

Example 1 (four steps) – three alternative design ideas are inspired by narrative springboards; words (*re-order and reflect*; *intensify and focus*; *drift and float*) are used to trigger spatial design ideas for a proposed urban-infill, mixed-use complex.

Example 2 (four steps) – three alternative spatial diagrams driven by word-gaming, expressing qualities and attributes desired for a new beachside development and water-taxi pier; the design ideas are inspired by three sets of narrative springboards (*wind, playful, and smart*; *sun, vigorous, and forceful*; *waves, springy, and bouncy*).

Example 2

In Example 2, the base drawing illustrates a new recreational beachside development, including watersports retail and rental services, concession buildings, along with a new pier to host a proposed water-taxi service. The new development will serve a diverse group of public users, integrating the local community with tourists and guests in a lakeside resort setting.

This design exploration can be accomplished by an individual or by a design team. In a team setting, the group can determine a long list of words – the amplifying descriptors. In this example an early meeting with the client resulted in the design team receiving a narrative statement: "The new beach development should be a lively community space that celebrates the beauty of our lake." This statement provided the team with a basis to invent their own descriptors to fuel the search for fresh design ideas for the project.

Example 2 demonstrates three design explorations, each of which is guided by three words. Two of the words express intangible sensations, design performance qualities, much like those in Example 1. But in this case a third word has been added to expresses a dynamic natural force operating at the site. The qualitative words were paired: *animated* and *wonderful*; *playful* and *smart*; *shiny* and *dazzling*; *springy* and *bouncy*; *sparkling* and *spirited*; *breezy* and *vibrant*; *brilliant* and *clear*; *delicate* and *graceful*; *vigorous* and *forceful*; *amazing* and *purposeful*; *bubbly* and *luminous*. Words expressing natural forces and conditions included: *sun, sand, moisture, winds, waves,* and *scents*.

As in Example 1, the base (given) diagram was drawn first in the left of four frames. It includes diagrammatic symbols highlighting the three natural-force words selected for each design exploration: *wind, sun,* and *waves*. Three additional frames were prepared in which to perform the design explorations. Then the natural-force expressions and qualitative words were chosen and assigned to guide each exploration, in the expectation that they would heighten and amplify the search for design ideas.

In the provided example, the first exploration selected a natural force and design qualities expressed as "*wind, playful, and smart.*" The second explored the ideas of "*sun, vigorous, and forceful.*" The third worked with the qualities of "*waves, springy, and bouncy.*"

The three resulting design explorations in this example illustrate diagrammatic design ideas for the project. The images denote distinctive alterations to the proposed (given) built forms and building footprints. The word-driven explorations also discovered ordering systems for the lakeside development that are more expressive of the natural systems and forces at play on the site. The design ideas demonstrate forms that are expressive of water movement, wave action, winds, incoming sun energy, and water–beach interface dynamics. These explorations also discover alternatives for the pier. Illustrated in the three explorations are configurations for the pier that reciprocate with the lake's wave and wind patterns, while also contributing an ordering system to the entire beachside development.

EXERCISE 2: THE SITE SPEAKS – NATURAL FEATURES REVEAL DESIGN IDEAS

This design exploration utilizes a less structured method than Exercise 1. It demonstrates the final exploration image in a representational form (perspective) rather than a diagrammatic depiction. This type of exploration is achieved with higher-resolution drawing techniques, and enhanced with colored-pencil rendering.

Step 1: a panoramic view of the natural site is sketched; landform, vegetative forms, and interrelationships are recorded. Step 2: design patterns are gleaned, abstracted, and extracted from the original site sketch, redrawn in new arrangements, interrelating site attributes in a kaleidoscopic impression.

Final design idea: patterns discovered and portrayed in Steps 1 and 2 impart forms and ordering systems as applied to the design exploration for a proposed community center complex and its entry/arrival landscape.

In this example, a proposed community center complex is sited amid a visually rich wilderness landscape. The example proceeds with the principle that natural landscape settings produce messages to both designers and eventual users. These nature-perceived messages or callings are very helpful in discovering site-sensitive design ideas for a proposed landscape. The design exploration utilizes quick, idealized sketches of the site's physical and natural attributes to seek and suggest design ideas for real project work. Natural landscapes are brilliant communicators of design possibilities. Through observation and sketching, natural traits convey spatial principles, forms, and patterns that inspire design options.

In this example, the first and second steps are accomplished on one sketchbook page; then a design exploration, a design idea, is drawn on a second page.

REFERENCES

Bandura, A. *Social Learning Theory*. Englewood Cliffs, NJ: Prentice Hall, 1977.

Hall, E. T. *The Silent Language*. New York: Doubleday, 1959.

Hall, E. T. *The Hidden Dimension*. New York: Doubleday, 1966.

Hall, E. T. *Beyond Culture*. New York: Doubleday, 1976.

DISCOVERING THE ARTISTRIES AND CRAFTS: BUILDING DESIGN LANGUAGE

5

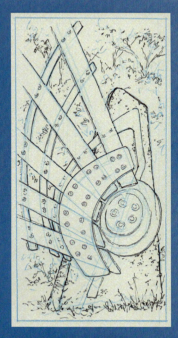

Synopsis: This chapter illustrates the use of drawing explorations that enrich the design development phase of projects. Demonstrated are design study techniques that cultivate design alternatives in more detail. The explorations generate ideas on how to articulate and express a design concept in greater detail. Drawing-based explorations readily populate the design process with imagery, enlivening the search for constructible forms. The explorations utilize narratives and metaphors as springboards to detect and illustrate particular patterns, geometries, shapes,

Design exploration considering foundation pier and bracketing for acentric fan-shaped arbor construct, expressing cyclical performance of natural systems.

and structural elements that are helpful in outfitting a design concept with meaningful details.

Primary learning outcome(s): By the end of this chapter, students will be able to produce a project-specific "design library" illustrating design component alternatives (shapes, geometries, structural frameworks, etc.) while fleshing out a site design. As a result, they will become more facile and inventive during the schematic and design-development stages of a project.

Relevance to landscape architectural students and professionals: Frequently, landscape architectural professionals, once they reach the schematic and design-development phases, experience pressure to finish the project quickly. Projects may come close to exceeding their design-phase budget (time and expense). This stress may cause designers, or entire project teams, to resort to short-cuts to achieve project closure. At this juncture, design detailing may shift to habitual, cut-and-paste methods, risking the abandonment of expression, losing hold of the rich and well-considered design intent.

BIG IDEAS MEET THEIR FINER POINTS

Fruitful design ideas have a way of confirming themselves. They generate enthusiasm and eagerness within the designer, an eagerness to learn and see more. A design idea marked with clarity and promise strikes chords, it signals to the designer that it is time to extend the search in greater detail. It declares that the delight in the design is just beginning to unfold. Design ideas buzzing with potential rouse a need to stretch the pursuit, to consider how the concept might hit the ground, become tangible, touchable, real.

When a design concept is ready for its buildable form, the designer enters another phase of discovery. A lively design concept calls out. It needs to find and confirm its companion elements, its design family. At this stage, the designer's joy is to gather the gear, the features that will craft the design's message and furnish its guiding principles. This phase of design introduces the design to its life. It discovers, then animates, the substance, the form, the structure, the

Design exploration – study of native plant form (sedges, reeds, and rushes) generates design ideas of geometric patterns to configure a wetland interpretation space.

---

flesh, the face – the heart of the design. It leads the design vividly towards real space and time, towards the built work.

This meeting of idea and tangible expression goes beyond a search for look, appearance, and materiality. At this point the designer is summoned to wonder, pondering ways to realize – to actualize – the design concept. The designer revisits the purposes and seeks out the means to accomplish the design's intents in stirring ways. This is the juncture where design probes deeper, discerning the qualities and values that will evoke and deliver meaning and message. This is a design phase not described in a project statement or contract for services. It is the phase that discovers a design's storyline before the script is set. It is time to generate schemes and formats before encumbering the design with "things and stuff." It is time to bolster the design idea, clothing it with authenticity and rich identity, preparing a landscape to be fitted with vivid experiences, resounding with expression.

A good design, a good landscape, is a performer and a performance. The audience comprises users, the occupants. They are recipients of the gifts of a landscape, especially the meaning, the understanding of the place – its story and messages. Landscapes generate impressions that fashion and clothe their users with remarkable experiences – encounters rich in information, learning, and impressions. By wondering how a design, a landscape, actually delivers this package of value and worth, the outfitting – the rigging of design – is revealed.

Design exploration – imagining orthogonal pavement fractured and dissolving applied to storm-water detention and bio-swale filtration functions (inspired by natural limestone pavement formations in Malham Cove, Yorkshire Dales, UK).

HOMECOMING – THE ART AND SCIENCE PARTNERSHIP

There are, of course, pre-packaged sources and solutions to bring reality to a design idea (e.g. design detailing catalogs, time-saving standards documents, etc.). But permitting habitual practices and templates to manifest a design concept will inevitably snuff out the brilliance of the big idea. The art residing in a rich idea is threatened when convention and routine-driven techniques prevail. Guiding a design concept towards buildability should result in increasing the spirit and vitality of the design. Transforming a good design into a valuable built-work requires great care. Watchfulness is necessary to keep alive the virtues of the concept as the design is formalized and detailed. The artistry in a design is nurtured as the science and technique of making are intertwined with lively imagination.

Artists, design professionals, and, for that matter, all those who endeavor to present beauty and inspiration for the benefit of others credit their effectiveness to abiding by a set of principles. They remain attentive to several fundamental responsibilities. They frame their work as an act of service. They closely follow the inspiration they initially encountered. Then, throughout an inventive and industrious process, they watch for, guide, and guard the details of the work.

These principles resonate with a charge of duty – the calling of the artist to the art. There are needs to sustain liveliness, alertness, and vigilance in the artist and in the methods. The craft of built landscapes is not realized by affixing templates to assemble form and space. The craft of place-making does not grow out of a material pick-and-choose session. There are intermediary layers of the design process that bridge and unify the gap between concept and construction.

Design exploration – visualizing entry gate panels to an orchard facility; abstract pattern derived from traits, natural forms, and geometries observed in a nut-tree grove (sunlight, branching, rolling landform, fruit shape, etc.).

120 DISCOVERING THE ARTISTRIES AND CRAFTS

When it is time to discover the particulars or elements that are true to the design idea, the features that are to unite to compose a built landscape, issues similar to those that confront an artist emerge. The artist sees an idea-in-mind, then begins the next process – presenting that idea outward as imagery on a canvas. The painter now engages and interacts in the physical realm. Painting is physical. The idea now gets its body. The idea gets its expression in actions as the artist literally *hands out* paint on canvas.

For the artist, at this bridge point, technique becomes the primary question and quest. Technique is a comprehensive interrelated set of variables. The artist administers systems of paint delivery to construct the image. The painter holds the original idea while expressing it via a performance involving arrays of interconnected, indeed interactive, options and choices. The choices are vast – media; texture of surface; brush size and type, bristle length, and strength; body posture; arm, wrist, hand position and gesture; force and pressure of application; values, intensities, and color palettes. Technique is an arbitrator and bridge. Technique gives idea its passage into view, into expression, into physical form. Originality in technique is what causes artistic expression, rewarding the idea with its finest and most moving countenance on the canvas.

Techniques, by definition, are methods and systems. Whether technique is applied to form art, to form music, or to form landscapes, fresh techniques, born of personal inquiry, connect invention and wit to venture well beyond the predictable, furnishing ideas with their genuine face.

> When you, body and soul, wish to make a certain expression and cannot be distracted from this one desire, then you will be able to make great use of whatever technical knowlecge you have . . . you will see the uses of techniques you already have, and you will invent more.
>
> (Henri 1923: 125)

Design exploration – image of a contemplative garden space configured with layered and intersecting elements, including rigid wall segments and tree lines that relax and soften to frame a watercourse and pool feature.

BEYOND THE USUAL

In *The Art Spirit* (1923), the American painter and teacher Robert Henri (1865–1929) offers thoughts on how to gain liberation from the habits and traditions that had long institutionalized artists, artistry, and art. Compiled by Margery Ryerson, the book includes a selection of Henri's notes, articles, letters, and advice to both students and colleagues. These fragments of an inspired career display Henri's passion and forceful encouragements, charging that art and science are vitalized and advanced by wonder and by wondering. He desired, above all, that his students develop keen curiosity and acquire an enduring flair for spontaneity in their work. He pressed them to sustain alertness and attentiveness at the critical point when ideas are transfigured into image. Henri insisted that his students were agile in thought and experimental in their attitude in advance of generating their work: "Get the principle of it, but not the mannerism" (Henri 1923: 127).

122   DISCOVERING THE ARTISTRIES AND CRAFTS

Through his notes, articles, and lectures, Henri demonstrates that his purpose was to stimulate individuals – and not only artists – to engage in independent thought, inquiry, and bold actions. Throughout the book he reiterates that his notions are not mandates to becoming a great artist. In fact, he expresses excitement that his provisions will generate divergent and contradictory points of view. With his invitation for alternative views comes his hope to stimulate the growth of originality and healthy diversity. He encourages all to delve into the benefits born of wondering. He expresses certainty that, as one is keen to question and speculate, one grows to be a fulfilled individual, capable of making great contributions to others – not only through their art, but also through their generously informed and fruitful lives.

> There are moments in our lives, there are moments in a day, when we seem to see beyond the usual. Such are the moments of our greatest happiness. Such are the moments of our greatest wisdom. If one could but recall his vision by some sort of sign. It was in this hope that the arts were invented. Sign-posts on the way to what may be. Sign-posts toward greater knowledge . . .
>
> (Henri 1923: 13)

> When the artist is alive in any person, whatever his kind of work may be, he becomes an inventive, searching, daring, self-expressing creature. He becomes interesting to other people. He disturbs, upsets, enlightens, and he opens ways to better understanding. Where those that are not artists are trying to close the book, he opens it, shows there are still more pages possible.
>
> (Henri 1923: 15)

Henri taught and encouraged his students. He pointed them to spirited thought that leads to inspiration. He showed them how to become inspired. He compelled them to be inspiring to others. His instructions aid artists in establishing a search-and-discover mindset,

DISCOVERING THE ARTISTRIES AND CRAFTS   123

resulting in enjoyable, fulfilling lives, yielding work delivered with impact. His lessons prepare the designer of landscapes for this fulfillment and prosperity. His notions wisely guide the designer and their processes for designing landscapes. He confirms that designers will produce their best natural and social life-sustaining works as they keep fertile the dynamic and inseparable partnership of art and science to craft good works. The genesis of powerful and sustaining design is located where imagination is interwoven with technique.

> The whole fact is that art and science are so close akin that they might very well be lumped together. They are certainly necessary to each other and the delights of either pursuit should satisfy any man.
>
> (Henri 1923: 54)

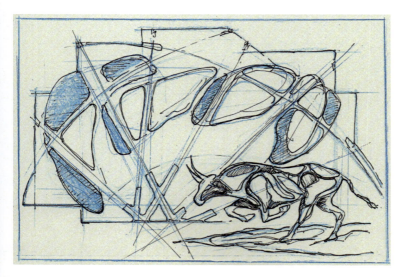

Design exploration – contour sketch of stampeding oxen highlights muscular groupings delivering impressive power in motion; the sketch elicits a second drawing of an imaginary construct expressive of mass, drive, and force.

INNOVATION IN THE BUILD-OUT – ACCESSING EVIDENCE

Good design draws freshness from resources, from evidence. Landscape architecture draws guidance and inspiration from nature and its systems. Nature exhibits evidence; it submits design ideas to the observant. Nature advocates for particular schemes to produce the detailing of built forms and completed works.

William Morris Hunt (1824–1879) was another American painter and art teacher. Henri credited Hunt's perspectives with influencing and shaping his own. He even quoted Hunt's teachings to generate debates and stimulate dialog among his students and colleagues.

Regardless of what his students chose as subject matter for artistic expression, Hunt charged them to study, observe, sketch, and express attributes of nature continuously in order to remain sharp and expressive:

> You are trying to compose without knowledge! Get your impressions from Nature. Composition is simply a recollection of certain facts. No exaggeration can be stronger than Nature, for nothing is so strange as truth! It is wilder and more weird than fancy! Look to Nature for material, then use it as you have need . . .
>
> (Hunt 1976: 4)

> The artist is an interpreter of Nature. People learn to love Nature through pictures. To the artist, nothing is in vain; nothing beneath his notice. If he is great enough, he will exalt every subject which he treats.
>
> (Hunt 1976: 15)

Hunt shared a profound lesson, charging artists so convincingly to experiment, express, and practice their craft that they expect – indeed believe – that outcomes will surprise the artist and astound the viewer.

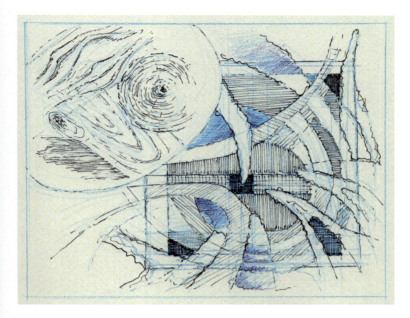

Design exploration – initial sketch records a variety of wood-grain patterns exposed from different saw-cut directions; second sketch imagines an intricate gathering space interweaving decking, unit paving, planting beds, and water features modeled after the grain patterns.

> There is force and vitality in a first sketch from life which the after-work rarely has. You want a picture to seize you as forcibly as if a man had seized you by the shoulder! It should impress you like reality!
>
> (Hunt 1976: 4)

Imagine Hunt and Henri overseeing a studio of aspiring landscape architects today. They would charge design students to investigate the technique, the artistry that will impart expression and meaning within a designed landscape. They would disallow mimicry or any habitual techniques to advance a design idea – no mannerisms. They would encourage the designer to invent fresh visual and spatial language. They would call for the birth of original techniques, novel frameworks to shape space and make the place. They would expect designs to be conversant with the site, bright with performance

DESIGN EXPLORATIONS – AWARENESS OF CRAFT

The previous design experiments and explorations have addressed the big picture, the approach, the overview or postures of an overall design. Generating design ideas at the next level of detail offers great rewards when thorough, when fueled by wondering.

At the moment when the design concept is ready for substance, form, flesh, and buildable directives, the designer enters the privileged point where techniques can be invented to achieve the design detailing – departing from pre-packaged sources and solutions. Uncovering physical attributes that may provide real expression of a design idea involves many design principles, including: geometric schemes; organizational patterns and arrangement; compositional patterns; negative and positive space frameworks; and visual figures and shapes.

These explorations can be illustrated by employing a number of different drawing conventions: plan view; eye-level and bird's-eye perspectives; profile and cross-section; and elevation.

The design explorations presented here demonstrate ways to prepare a varied design language to formulate and fulfill a design concept. They utilize a variation of the design library technique, introduced in Chapter 3. They demonstrate the selection of design components that merit *wondering* – investigating design techniques that could effectively and expressively contribute to an overall design intent.

These explorations purposely generate an array of optional design elements that will reinforce a site design concept and move the design forward with optional and fitting particulars or details. The explorations guide students in visually brainstorming – to form, shape, and craft optional means by which the landscape features and built structures of a site design can achieve the design's overarching intents with an awareness of artistry.

These techniques utilize narrative and visual metaphor to illustrate fashioning and fulfilling a design concept at the individual component level (e.g. spatial characteristics and framing; surfacing patterns; entry, path, and corridor conditions; boundary, edge, enclosure language).

The examples used art paper of medium-valued neutral background (ivory, tan, buff, etc.). With this medium, black and grey-scale ink images are amplified with the addition of colored-pencil rendering, including white and light-value highlights to increase the articulation of form and texture.

Design detailing explorations – illustrating an array of surfacing techniques (imagined and drawn) based on words and expressions signifying possible detailing characteristics and qualities, including: *dissolve, disassociate, and drift*; *yielding and reciprocating*; and *compression, release, exhale, and inhale*.

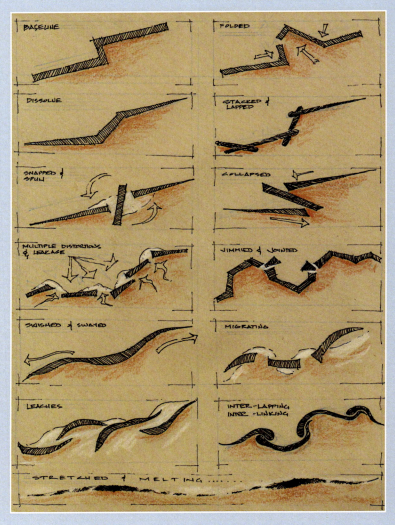

Design detailing explorations – illustrating an array of edge and boundary-making techniques (imagined and drawn) based on words and expressions signifying possible detailing characteristics and qualities, including: *folded*; *dissolve*; *stacked and lapped*; *snapped and spun*; *collapsed*; *distortions and leakage*; *jimmied and jointed*; *swished and swayed*; *migrating*; *leaches*; *inter-lapping and inter-linking*; *stretched and melting*.

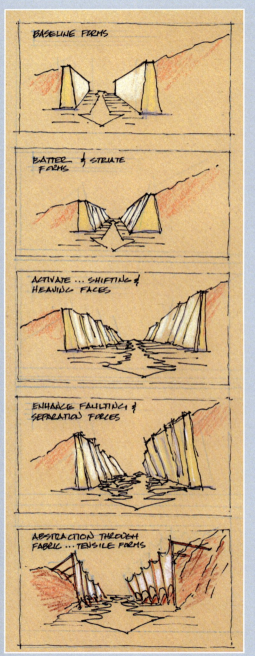

Design detailing explorations – illustrating a variety of ways to form a passage, endeavoring to emulate a natural canyon formation (imagined and drawn), based on words, expressions, and alternative materials to discover possible design detailing variations, including: *battered and striated forms*; *active, shifting, and heaving faces*; *enhanced faulting and separation forces*; *abstraction via fabrics and tensile forms*.

in support of the inhabitants, and perceptive in the expression of purpose, intent, and meaning. They would require wondering.

Wonder is associated with visual surprise or amazement. An enthusiastic sense of wonder leads to design discoveries, surprises, and images that draw attention and invite consideration. Wonder is fueled by alertness, triggering full and fervent investigation. To wonder is a decision to remain invigorated and empowered in thought – engaging the senses, expecting surprises that may strengthen a design's outcome. Wonder is especially vital as the designer reaches for the details and particulars to manifest the design in built form. Wonder takes place in a sporty atmosphere, entertaining pliable and expandable design thoughts. Wonder sneaks into the cracks between obvious and done before, revealing unique alternatives.

Socrates purportedly declared: "Wonder is the beginning of wisdom."

Wondering is a prized partner in expanding the language of design and its detailing. Wondering does not disregard the origin or the purpose of the original design idea. Wondering is not formless or detached. Wondering is a rubbing together, a honing and sharpening process – the original idea and the details sharpen and perfect each other. Wondering triggers sparks that leap from an idea to a design's concrete expression, the forms and patterns for sculpting the built-work. Wonder bypasses the gravity of habitual thinking and doing, stretching and reaching to grasp freshness of approach, yielding newness as a landscape hits the ground.

DESIGN IDEAS HIT THE GROUND – EXAMPLES OF DESIGN DETAILING EXPLORATIONS

The above examples explore a variety of ways that processes and movement could affect interpretation and therefore the look and performance of surfaces, boundaries, and spatial enclosure. The images are triggered in response to expressive words or phrases that align with and reinforce a dynamic design concept. These are examples of quick visual inventions. These drawing-based explorations bring forward possible landscape treatments, detailing elements that yield qualitative features and convey metaphoric expressions to support the original design concept.

REFERENCES

Henri, R. *The Art Spirit*. Boulder, CO: Westview Press, 1923.

Hunt, W. M. *On Painting and Drawing*. Mineola, NY: Dover Publications, 1976 (compilation of *Talks on Art, First Series* [1896] and *Talks on Art, Second Series* [1898]).

IDEAS FEED THE BUILD

6

Design exploration – an abstract process drawing, investigating a composition of shapes and lines that are introduced to migration and movement; new forms emerge based on the tendencies of original elements moving in and among each other, seeking conditions of balance and equilibrium.

Synopsis: This chapter presents examples of landscapes whose designs and final built forms were influenced by the explorative drawing techniques demonstrated in the previous chapters. Diagrammatic drawings are

juxtaposed with images of the constructed facilities, illustrating the influence of exploratory drawings on project outcomes. These projects were designed and constructed as a result of public–private partnerships, including the author as supervisor and landscape architect, interdisciplinary teams of students (primarily landscape architectural students), as well as expert constructors and engineers assisting as professional consultants and adjunct teachers. The design exploration examples were generated by the author in order to mentor students in the discovery of design ideas that yield distinctive built landscapes.

Primary learning outcome(s): By the end of this chapter, students will be able to appreciate and enjoy the practical value of employing design experiments and explorations to advance their own project work. Included in this outcome, students who continue to develop and employ these drawing-based experiments will develop confidence in their design process. They will establish more thorough design development methods, aware of their responsibility to practice and make ready a variety of fresh and new ideas in determining design possibilities in future projects. They will be able to personalize drawing-based ideation methods, adding vigor to their professional practice of landscape architecture. Adapting these techniques will increase students' capacity to contribute delightful, lively, and surprising built-works that will yield personal rewards while providing enriching benefits for the users they serve. Students will demonstrate increased awareness regarding how to promote symbiosis between the artistry of design and the science and technology of place-making.

Relevance to landscape architectural students and professionals: Landscape architectural students and professionals wish to deliver novel designs. Clients frequently require fast-track time lines for delivery of designs and built landscapes. Designers and design firms are challenged with profound costs and overheads in delivering designs, especially when progressing the work to a constructible stage. Simple, enjoyable, quick, and profitable design experimentation can resolve some of these pressures and constraints, while increasing the likelihood of achieving award-worthy designs and built results.

IDEAS, IMPROVISATION, DRAWING

A spirited built landscape ascends from the idea that imagined it. The path to discover the fruitful design is diverse, varied, and thorough. Accomplishing the compelling buildable design is the result of wide-ranging efforts of individuals participating within a cohesive team. A comprehensive design process engages many experts and contributors who employ diverse tools, techniques, and thought processes.

Exploratory drawing is a crucial and generous contributor within this alliance. Drawings, and the probing that is activated while drawing, contribute in distinct ways to design discovery. Drawings are unique participants in the design team. They are quick to generate and versatile in reaching towards more resolute design decisions. Experimental drawings, when included in all stages of a design process, provide layer upon layer of possible design outcomes. A single drawing charts a flood of thoughts. The designer applies a tactile push and pull of pencil and pen across paper. A simple

Design exploration – visualizing a radially segmented landform intended as a land laboratory learning station, affording visitors the experience of solar radiation and thermal output as a function of varied slope angles and differing solar orientation.

IDEAS FEED THE BUILD   135

drawing, searching out a design, fabricates imagery teeming with questions, insight, and keys that are relevant to the project.

Drawings utilized to advance a design from its idea to its constructs bring the value of improvisation to the work of design. Improvisational learning is effectively used as a tool for discovery in many artistic, scientific, cognitive, and organizational management disciplines. Improvization is not an act of frolicking. It is not boundary-less. It is not winging it. Improvisation avails open and interactive search-and-find processes, achieved with balance and order. It is a discovery tool that supplies meaningful results. When used to accomplish design explorations, improvisational drawing methods promote spontaneity of expression while remaining carefully tethered to the principles founded in the design concept.

Improvisation, when describing a way of drawing, is comparable to a conversation. In human interactions involving language and discourse, dialog builds in an exchange, an encounter. In most conversations the participants engage in give and take. They each cycle through phases. Partners in a conversation alternate between the roles of contributor and listener. When conversing, one adds to, counters, or even diverts the conversation in a different direction. As a team, the two participants are improvising. They are continually building and expanding upon previous points they have each offered. Generally, a conversation runs its course and concludes. The participants, by trading back and forth, have conferred, considered, deliberated, and consulted with each other. They have, through reciprocal contributions, built an experience, an event – a relationship with an outcome. However, the outcome of a conversation is not necessarily conclusive, sealed, and terminated. An outcome resulting from dialog typically remains open for further consideration. The outcome lives on as a building block for the next encounter – the next conversation. Improvisation, as conversation, discovers and establishes some points of closure or structure, while generating anticipation for future exchange, continuation, and growth in the matter.

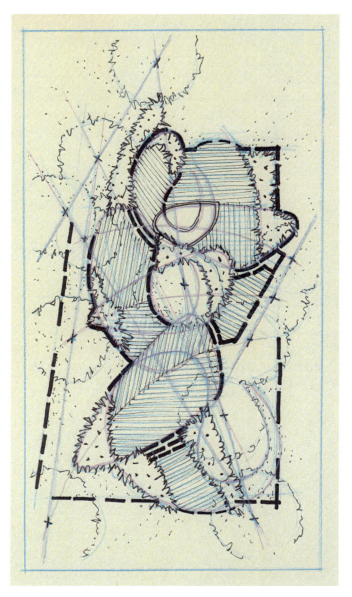

Design exploration – a form-finding experiment based on a family of six shapes, each arranged on straight or arced vectors (purple-colored shapes and lines). The initial shapes and lines were used as base geometries to discover and scribe a plan view of a small enclosed garden, composed of intricate sub-spaces and level changes, and framed with low walls, planting masses, and canopy tree arrangements.

IDEAS FEED THE BUILD

As in a conversation, an exploratory design drawing stimulates a productive give and take. The imagery builds line-by-line, shape-by-shape, and tone-by-tone. As it builds, it invites, evokes, more avenues for interjection. The drawing-in-progress seems ever malleable. The imagery that was laid down just moments before provokes new moves, motivating the designer to improvise more, to expand the drawing through interpolation, extrapolation, and modification.

Imparting artistry in a design process requires practice. Improvisational drawings produce a distinct type of practice. Practicing artistry, for designers, is a performance, a balancing act – a curious troupe that blends entertainment, impulse, concentration, and deliberation. Design experimentation serves

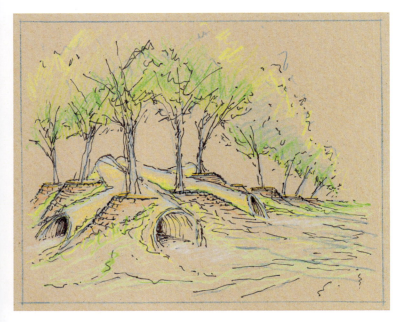

Design exploration – visualizing a ruin-like space, presenting tumbled tubular passages, crawling landforms, and vining groundcover plantings, woven among battered, rustic stone tree planters (design idea generated while sketching ruins overtaken by trees at Preah Khan Temple, Angkor, Cambodia).

as a fruitful collaborator, a teammate contributing to accountable and comprehensive design outcomes. An art-based approach in generating design ideas prevents a designer's work from becoming preordained or prescriptive. The ways a designer chooses to practice, experiment, and explore design possibilities develop from a personal calling. A design process that is governed excessively by one principle, premise, bias, or false sense of constraint can readily become imbalanced and incomplete.

EXAMPLES OF DESIGN EXPLORATIONS INFORMING BUILT-WORKS

The drawing techniques demonstrated in this chapter were performed with anticipation, expecting useful results. The images formed in these design explorations were attentive to site attributes and natural systems, while carefully considering programmatic needs, as expressed by clients and users. These projects were charged with providing outdoor recreation opportunities concurrent with wildlife habitat enhancement. The images provide examples of improvisational drawings that triggered visions for the built-works. They comprise visual pathways, aiding the search for and illumination of design possibilities for real places. The conceptual drawings emerged from enthusiasm, from personal initiative, from believing that artistry in design is essential in generating distinctiveness in built-works.

The following examples reveal that drawing-based design explorations play a key role in directing final designs for constructed landscapes. They provide evidence that drawing explorations lead to expressive forms and fulfillment of functional requirements, while evoking the aesthetic values coded in original design ideas. Employing these exploratory drawing techniques delivered spatial principles, ordering systems, landform, layout, structural forms, and engineering principles that ultimately guided the detailed design of the built-works.

The drawings demonstrate the cumulative application of several design experiments and drawing exploration techniques that were discussed earlier in this book. They reveal how a number of the exercise methods practiced in previous chapters can be united, integrated, and interwoven to produce a medley of imagery that guides the final design of complex landscapes.

These cases exclude many design-development studies and technical drawings that directed construction detailing and build-out later in the design process. The purpose of these examples is to illustrate the potency of the diagrammatic experiments and design explorations in providing substance and articulation to final designs and completed forms.

A NATURE AREA AND COUNCIL RING

A cultural center campus features a museum, exhibition hall, formal gardens, and nature learning area. The nature area was achieved by reclaiming a long-abandoned six-acre (approx. 2.5-hectare) gravel mine. The nature facility hosts environmental education programs for public schools in the region. The master plan for the area designated a loop-trail system, passing through representative and recreated ecozones native to the region. The zones included tall-grass prairie openings; scrub/shrub successional zones and mesic-deciduous woodland; and ephemeral and open-water wetlands. Learning and activity spaces were sited along the loop trail, including: a council ring and amphitheater; a terraced rain garden sector for water-quality management and habitat enhancement; an open-water and wetland observation pier; a bird blind; a storytelling and craft-activity nook; a woodland canopy-level observation point; and an overlook at the site's highest elevation, providing a space for review of and reflection on completed nature lessons at a vantage point with views of all ecozones.

One signature space within the nature facility is highlighted in this example: the council ring, which is enveloped by a small amphitheater. The facility's program calls for group visitors to arrive, walk a short portion of the trail, gradually descending in elevation through the prairie zone, then sit in a space conducive for introductory lessons and instructions. After the full group orientation at the council ring, sub-groups are formed and dispersed to other (smaller) learning spaces for lessons and hands-on activities.

The form and spatial arrangement for the council ring and amphitheater became an important design question. The nature area's initial meet-and-greet space – an impression-setting staging area – needed to demonstrate a key landscape architectural principle: that functional configuration can grow out of the native landscape and its characteristic forms and functions. This principle – *of* the land, not *on* it – influenced the conceptual diagramming of the amphitheater space as a nest. The design explorations discovered opportunities for the staging area to tuck away from the trail, like an eddy or a fold. The sketches helped to visualize the space as a ground nest, shouldered by the prairie, shaped by the trail's descent.

Early inspirations for the design explored a concept highlighting movement and flow. The flow of a prairie carpet expressing breezes and winds, the flow of water interlacing the site (surface and sub-surface), and the flow of visitors into a casual assembly for their introductory course of study all emerged as valued design influences. The principles and forms associated with the idea of flow provided a bond for the design – a *parti* with promise.

This composite design exploration revealed distinctive land-formation possibilities for the gathering space, while engaging other tiers of design thought. The drawing overlaid a number of diagrammatic references to natural systems that were important to the functions and environmental performance of the council ring. The patterns of surface water flowing across the land were indicated. Shallow sub-surface interflow, water trending downhill out of view, beneath the slope shouldering the amphitheater, was represented in the plan- and section-view imagery. Vectors drawn to represent direct sunlight input (diurnal and seasonal sun patterns) further prompted acentric form notions to the space.

[Note: The experimental and exploratory drawing techniques used here have been illustrated and described in Chapters 1, 2, 4, and 5, as well as earlier in this chapter.]

The exploratory drawing contributed guidance to the design and significantly influenced the resulting build-out of the gathering space. The interactions of flow, sun paths, slope gradients, and water movement were married in one interlaced diagram. A spiraling eddy, intercepting descending runs of water and splayed to invite diurnal and seasonal sunlight variations, was expressed in the layered composition. The amphitheater took shape – a terraced acentric swirl, focusing and compressing in the core.

Design exploration – a composite sketch, exploring forms expressing *flow*, useful for finding forms and design language for the amphitheater and council-ring space.

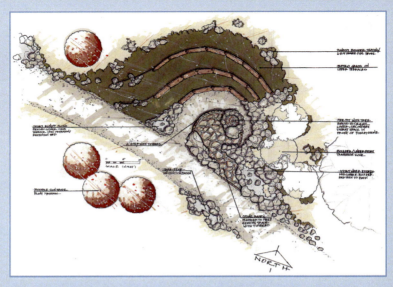

Master plan for the amphitheater and council-ring space.

Timber crib framework that furnished seating terraces and bench forms, while allowing groundwater interflow to continue its natural movement out of view and beneath, eventually daylighting in a small retention pool at the edge of the stage platform.

The terracing was accomplished with native timber crib walls, battered to provide restful benches and seat backs for users. The cribs were backfilled with native coble and gravel, providing a hidden conduit for surface water and shallow interflow to flow behind the walls, reappearing to daylight in a rain garden enveloping the central stage. The wide-to-narrowed terrace rows perform well to group visitors in a comfortable assembly. The funneled form gathers students inward from the trail, to the nest of seats. The arced ledges also provide options for groups to adjust their sitting position in relation to sun angles and passive heating conditions. During chilly spring and fall meetings, students naturally choose to sit in the compressed terrace section, snug and close to the stage core, remaining warm and comfortable for the lesson.

The amphitheater and council ring as constructed.

A NEIGHBORHOOD POCKET PARK AND COMMUNITY GREENWAY REST STOP

A regional rails-to-trails greenway walking and bicycle system passes through urban areas. A portion of the pathway occurred beside a neighborhood that had no nearby park space. As a result, the greenway proprietors partnered with the municipal park system to develop a small parcel, transforming it into a rest stop on the greenway while providing a pocket park for the adjacent community.

The project presented opportunities to highlight the greenway as a valuable recreational and wellness amenity, especially by providing better access from the bordering neighborhood. This new addition to the trail focused on drawing families and youth from the nearby high school to use and interact with the greenway opportunities. The adjoining sidewalks were separated from the greenway by a very steep rise. The greenway was elevated approximately eight feet (2.5 meters) above the street level. It was apparent that pedestrians and bicycle users needed a ramped-cut, through the slope, in order to provide accessible passage from street level up to the park. It was clear that a cut-through would provide needed visual access, too.

The modest-sized space allotted for the rest stop and park node connected to the greenway at a bend in the trail. The community expressed the need for a plaza space to host gatherings for family-sized celebrations, neighborhood cookouts, and small impromptu performances. Citizens expressed a desire to meet freely and greet greenway trail users if they elected to pause in the park for a break.

Considerations that stimulated early design explorations emphasized that this park needed to declare itself. The forms and spatial patterns needed to cue an invitation visually by motioning walkers and cyclists to accept the offer to move into a cove, an eddy beside the greenway strand. The diagramming experimented with placing the park/plaza very near to the trail – almost on the trail and intersecting it. This reinforced the expressed desire for the park to join the greenway path, not to be an appendage or amendment, not to be isolated or separated.

This design exploration imagery illustrates a greeting, a meeting, a union. This example demonstrates the use of layered diagramming that discovers forms interacting and dovetailing with one another. The imagery conveys a meeting and a moment in time. The diagram communicates an idea of two friends coming together, expressing great care for one another. The image captures a frame in which trail and park unite, find each other. The union affects a swell that excites ripples and sprays. The drawing poses an ellipse at the epicenter of

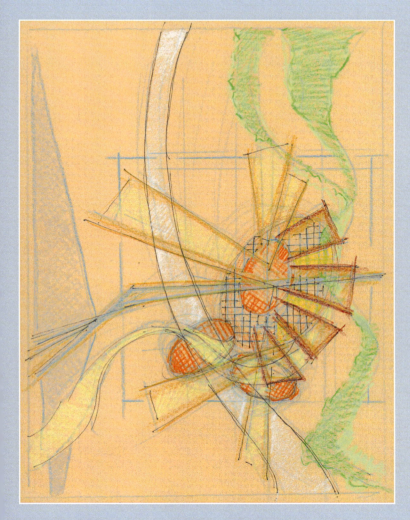

Design exploration – a diagram expressing qualities for the new rest-stop park space integrated with the existing greenway hiking/running/biking trail. Qualities desired for the space included: *beckon*, *reach out*, *invite*, *meet*, *greet*, *gather*, *collaborate*, and *bridge*; an eddy form was discovered to be helpful in conveying many of these qualities.

the interaction, marking the encounter of path and space. Slices or rays stretch, reach, and radiate outward – toward the neighborhood and woodland. Other rays extend across, grasping and bridging the trail. This design study makes evident spatial configurations and forms that will contribute to the purpose of the park – to unite community members by serving local neighborhood and greenway users concurrently.

[Note: The exploratory drawing technique used here has been illustrated and described in Chapters 4 and 5.]

The principle of beckoning activates reciprocal forces, drawing in while radiating and reaching out. This project-based design exploration discovered forms and patterns that express union and collaboration. The imagery conveys attributes of emitting and gathering simultaneously. Diagramming these integral forces availed a primary design idea. Radially set frames mark a way, voice notice, and invite users into a rhythmic passage ascending from street to haven. The frames are portals and gates. They fashion a subtle net. They fix a filter for a new little park. They signal an invitation, calling together a new-found community, not two but one.

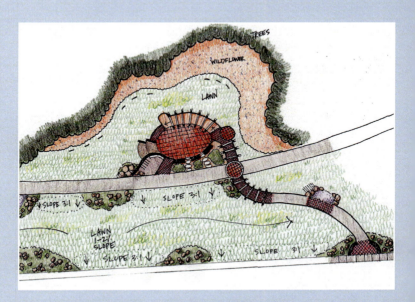

Master plan and photographs of the park space as constructed.

A WETLAND NATURE PRESERVE – HOME FOR HERONS AND AN ICONIC PAVILION

A public conservation facility was commissioned to recognize the former director of the municipal water-quality division. Selected for development was a 27-acre site (approx. 11 hectares) within the city limits. The site is adjacent to the city's defining water course, a once-pristine, then polluted, and now restored river. The honoree and his team of dedicated water-quality professionals returned the river to good health during an intense 25-year clean-up initiative. The river corridor, traversing through the city and county, has become the focus of community trail networks, passive recreation overlooks, public fishing, and watersports recreation.

A majority of the site is in the flood plain of a river that played an important role for pre-settlement Indians and continues to do the same for a town that has grown to become predominantly industrial in economy. The site is at the edge of town, just within the city limits. The parcel was undeveloped and gifted to a municipal entity by a defunct industry. The site had hosted some low-intensity agricultural production in its recent past, making it a good candidate for riparian habitat rehabilitation.

The project required an internal trail and boardwalk network, spaces for arrival and staging of student groups visiting for environmental education purposes. The master plan also called for a variety of spaces (stations) situated on the trail and boardwalk system to host interpretive lessons specific to the variety of ecosystems to be recreated on the site. The facility was also required to perform as naturalized parkland, open to the public for wildlife observation and general enjoyment year round. Public-use and larger group-education functions required a larger gathering space housed within a pavilion. The clients asked that the pavilion be of exemplary design, providing a memorable visual impact for users of the site. It should be an icon for the preserve.

Early in the design ideation process, the neighboring riparian wildlife species became a subject of interest and inquiry. Optimizing the passive recreation and environmental education purposes required plans to regenerate habitats for wildlife species, to extend homes for nearby species, and to attract new species. Learning about and appreciating the wildlife users of the site would clearly provide promising and fresh design ideas for the pavilion space. It was anticipated that nature's users of the site, their habits, and their patterns of movement could inspire ordering systems design language for the site's learning stations and support structures.

The design objectives set for the site included recreating wetland systems to emulate pre-settlement performance. Meeting this objective entailed minor landform modifications to promote a larger open-water basin, allowing the site to host a sizeable water body through the majority of an annual cycle. The open-water attribute was important for attracting and sustaining raptors and wading birds. A number of hawk species were common in the area. Eagles and ospreys had been returning to the region for several years. Eagles were already nesting within a few miles of the site.

Although not typical residents of local wetlands, cranes had recently been spotted staging nearby for short stays during their migration. With water-basin improvements on the site, the project anticipated hosting cranes for such temporary stays. Expectations for increased sightings of local and migrating wetland birds began stimulating design ideas that drew upon the characteristics of wading birds. Water birds interacting with shallow-water wetlands began to inspire the design of built structures at the water's edge.

Of all the wading birds driving specific habitat restoration, the great blue heron rose to prominence. Herons were common visitors to the section of river adjacent to the site. They had established rookeries within a mile

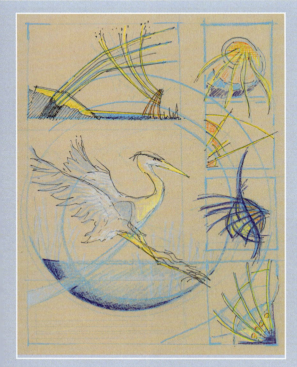

Design exploration – a composite sketch, generating gesture images, idealized cross-sections, and plan-view diagrams; each is an abstract impression of action and movement displayed by the heron at the moment of landing.

(1.6 kilometers). Witnessing these magnificent birds at close range, especially during water landings, affirms their title – *great*. Other titles and equally valid descriptors might include *grand*, *splendid*, and *noble*. The scope of the bird is remarkable, its spread and size not detracting from stunning delicacy and grace.

Two drawings were influential in generating the final design of the pavilion. The first was a composite drawing, starting with a sketch of a great blue heron, moments before landing. The action sketch of the heron then inspired a series of form-finding images (plans, sections, and elevations) for the pavilion. Together, these images explored impressions of flight, take-off, and landing, and of the water that becomes energized and active when bird and water excite each other.

[Note: The experimental and exploratory drawing techniques used here have been illustrated and described in Chapters 1, 2, 4, and 5, as well as earlier in this chapter.]

The second design exploration evolved from the first. It became more representational, more three-dimensional. It expressed ideas for the pavilion in which the structural framework emulated patterns observed in the heron's touchdown. In what could be interpreted as a section or elevation view, a

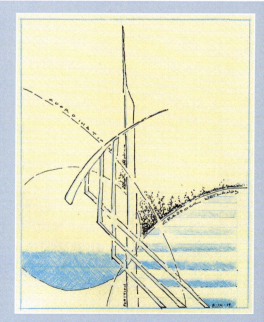

Design exploration – a second drawing that extracts qualities of the initial design exploration and visualizes a literal form possibility for the pavilion.

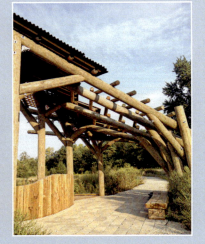

Photographs of the pavilion as constructed.

pavilion form was inspired by the movement vectors associated with the wings in the moment of braking. Though landing, the bird's wings are partnering with the air mass, above and below, to generate lift that effectively controls the fall. The drawing exploration also interlaces imagery derived from the heron's long-limbed nature, its light touch and interaction with water, reeds, and rushes punctuating the wetlands, and gestures that reach up to and acknowledge the sky above.

[Note: The exploratory drawing technique used here has been illustrated and described in Chapters 4 and 5.]

A heron landing is an event, a dance. The bird is entirely unfolded, wings stretched, falling with loft, grasping a full cushion of air, long legs reaching and bracing, alighting, scarcely displacing water upon touchdown. The diagramming of this dance shaped the pavilion's built form. Design-drawing techniques contributed greatly to establishing the pavilion's light appearance. The drawings helped to discover the pavilion's long-lasting posture, its structural equilibrium, by applying counterbalance engineering. The structure reached, arching up and forward, posing the fading of flight and the instant of landing. The layered seating suggests gentle impact – the rippling of water – not a disturbance, but notes of arrival.

CONCLUSION 7

In ancient Rome, Vitruvius proclaimed that designers are commissioned to effect good design. He provided enduring lessons, urging designers to find and perfect their designs with vigor. His main message was not so much what to do to reach the optimum design, but how it is readily recognized when it is achieved. He described good design from the perspective of what it looks like, the sensations it produces, and how it guides the built outcome to perform well – serving users with necessary functions amidst gracefulness and beauty. Good design is insightful and serviceable – packaged in discovery, delight, and surprise (Vitruvius 1960).

With his admonitions for good design, and his clues that help identify it, Vitruvius continues to offer designers timely and meaningful encouragement. He exhorts them to search freely well beyond the obvious in the expectation of discovering the astonishing design. The anticipation of bright discoveries generates unlimited incentive to push further in the process that delivers the design, stretching to apply a broad and ever-expanding array of techniques to keep the search fresh, alive, and productive. There is no prescription for good design, but the designer moving forward, fueled with expectation, is assured that it is attainable and deliverable.

154   CONCLUSION

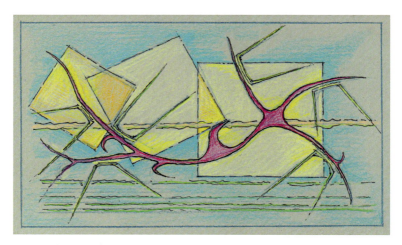

Design exploration – diagrammatic sketch exploring the aggressive growth and tenacious forces demonstrated by roots and rhizomes penetrating and pushing inert objects.

Design students and professionals are refreshed when a design idea begins to "spark and sizzle." An energetic design idea is invigorating, alive with hope, and destined to impart innovation. Quickness and pace, while generating design ideas, position the designer as inventor – bright with awareness, animated and effective in the work. Promoting the use of experimental drawings to find and express design ideas does not exclude other valued methods for doing so. But the act of drawing and the images produced have proven through the ages to be highly profitable in the quest for imaginative designs.

Drawings are resource efficient – the time taken, effort expended, energy used, and materials required are minimal, simple, and accessible. The process of drawing, when freed up for the purpose of discovery, unfastens the designer from preordained conclusions and data-driven devices. Drawings are viewable from limitless perspectives and points of view. A drawing may instigate a volley of interpretations simultaneously. Exploratory drawings generate graphic impulses, inducing visual alertness in the designer. They relax the designer, nourishing versatility in thought.

CONCLUSION   155

Producing a drawing is a bodily event, inviting the designer's eyes to sense real space and real time. Drawings are tactile visual tools that physically connect the designer to a path of design inquiry. Sometimes the inquiry eagerly leads the designer to see a design. Other times the inquiry triggers new questions, leading the design search elsewhere, onto a fresh path filled with surprises. A simple experimental drawing kindles a pictorial episode, fostering clues, offering release from the rational, arousing intuition. Intuition generates the scent, the trail that leads to discovery.

Throughout this book, the examples of design experimentation and exploration have addressed a realm, one aspect of drawing-base design discovery warranting the designer's full attention. The practice of experimental drawing is a personal adventure. So, the techniques described herein should evolve into personalized methods. In the spirit of Robert Henri, the examples, the methods, and the instructions are not presented to promote conformity among students of design. Indeed, the examples should be used

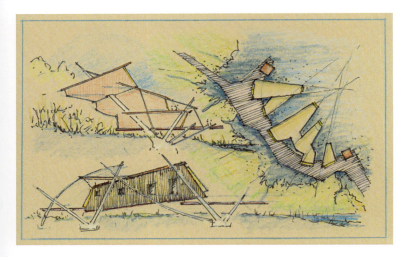

Design exploration – investigating low-impact and low-touch structural forms integrated at the edge of recreated wetland, imagining retreat structures to house visiting ecologists, researchers, and environmental artists, as well as laboratories, learning galleries, and environmental educational spaces.

CONCLUSION

Experimental sketch entitled *Angles of Resplendent Repose* – image drawn from memory and imagination, representing varied gradients of weathered landforms exposed on the windward side of a Caribbean island.

CONCLUSION   157

as springboards. Consider and follow them *up to a point*, but then adapt, transform, and morph the techniques. Expect to discover personal approaches in the use of experimental drawing that diversify the practice of design.

In a complex and often perplexing world, designers, and their designs, have a responsibility to be at their best. Landscape architecture is a vital force, a service profession, partnering with a host of allied disciplines in this responsibility. The ideas, designs, and spaces built under the leadership of landscape architects are crucial. The scope of these responsibilities, the challenges, the threats and stresses on our landscapes may appear overwhelming. It is important, however, not to cede control to this sense of urgency. It should not be allowed to weigh down design thinking with "fix-it" tactics and solely technical solutions. Landscape architecture is especially revered for its assuring, calming, and spirited approaches to design. Rather than succumbing to the weight, landscape architects faithfully practice and perform a lively design process – light and airy on its feet.

This book presents a call to action for design students and professionals. Keep your sketchbooks active, electrified. Practice design regularly, anticipating joy. Provide generous space to the design process and populate it first with thrilling ideas, not weighty apprehensions. Consider the design process, the act of designing, as an open road – *wide open*. Then accelerate. As the thrill sinks in, hold fast to the discovery-rich heritage, the noble art, and the science of designing with and for the land.

REFERENCE

Vitruvius. *The Ten Books on Architecture*. Trans. Morris Hicky Morgan. Mineola, NY: Dover Publications, 1960 (first published 1914).

INDEX

action-oriented observations 90
addition 97
algebra 66, 67–8, 74
Alhambra (Granada, Spain) *64*
alternative design ideas *80–1, 111*
amphitheaters *141–3*
ancient burial sites *82*
Angles of Resplendent Repose 156
anthropological perspectives
    97–100
applied ecology 39
art and science partnership 3–5,
    118–20, 123
art-based approaches 138
Arthur's Seat (Edinburgh, Scotland) *5*
artistry 137–8
Art Spirit, The (Henri) 121
art structure catching rain *21*
astute observations 94
attention (observational learning)
    92
Avignon (France) *4*

Bandura, Albert 92–4, 96
Barcelona (Spain) *1*
blue-lines 21–2
built forms, and intersecting
    volumes *12*

Caribbean island land forms *156*
carriage sketches *75*
Cloud Gate sculpture (Millennium
    Park, Chicago) *89*
co-housing cluster study *24*
collage-style drawing *73*
community greenway rest stop
    144–7
computation 68
conch shell sketch *37*
contemplative garden space *121*
control 3
convention 118
council ring 140–3
creativity 11–12, 14, 32
critical patterns 38
cultural practices 97, 101

data mining 16–17
Davies Alpine House (Kew Gardens,
    London) *63*
design: art and science 5; as
    experimental 45; and planning
    principles *78 see also* field
    sketching
design aerobics exercises 24–5
design concepts 116–17, 118–20,
    126

design conversations 99, 135–7
design detailing explorations *127–9*
design discovery 11–13
design education 11–12, 96
designers, relationship with drawings 98–9
design exercises 88 *see also* exercises
design experiments 16–18, 46–7, 137–8, 155; low-impact and low-touch structural forms *155*; slowing storm waters *45*; village sketch *40*; water-harvesting pavilion form *73*
design exploration 16–18; art structure catching rain *21*; awareness of craft 126–9; contemplative garden space *121*; conversations 135–7; design tools 107–9; edge and boundary-making techniques *128*; entry gate panels *119*; equestrian competition facility *100*; form-finding experiment *136*; forming passages *129*; forms expressing flow *141*; gesture images *149*; informing built-works 138–9; inner precedents 105–7; interpretive center *93*; land-formation 141; low-impact and low-touch structural forms *155*; native calligraphic forms *102*; native plant forms *117*; orthogonal pavement *118*; radially segmented landform *134*; rest-stop park space 144–5; roots and rhizomes *154*; ruin-like space *137*; space-efficient and energy-conserving town *95*; stampeding oxen *123*; surfacing techniques *127*; terraced

landscapes *104*; transit-oriented development (TOD) *106*; wetland nature preserve *98*; wildlife habitat *90*; wood-grain patterns *125*
design force 39
design ideas 102–3, 110–13, 116
design innovation 103
design intervention 39, 45–6
design library 76–81
design objectives 148–9
design outcomes 103
design precedents 105
design process legislator 44
design readiness 8–9
design tools 107–9
design translation 77, 82–3
Design with Nature (McHarg) 39–45
development 38
drawing: as a bodily event 155; designer relationship with 98–9; exploratory 8, 134, 154; improvisation 135; resource efficient 154
drawing exercises 16, 21–4, 32–3
drawing-generated observation 88
drawing pursues design 6–7
duty 119

Eagle Creek Park (Earth Discovery Center, Indianapolis) *67*
ecology 39 *see also* natural systems
edge and boundary-making techniques *128*
Edinburgh, Scotland *5*
education and practice 6
Einstein, Albert 68–9
energetic design ideas 154
energy-conserving town *95*
equestrian competition facility *100*
evidence-based design 38

160   INDEX

exercises 19–20; design aerobics 24–5; design exercises 88; design library 76–81; design translation 82–3; form-finding 48–58; making design tools 107–8; migration 30–1; move, merge and mingle 28–9; round robin 26–7; word-gaming 110–13

experiences 91

experimental drawings: design intercession 47; design readiness 8; expressing design ideas 154; flexible spatial order *43*; human development and landform *46*; "living machine" at shoreline *15*; personal adventure 155–7; possible design outcomes 134–5; visual discussions 97–8

experimentation: exercises 19–20; and innovation 6; risk-taking 67; science and mathematics 16; side-by-side drawings 76–7

experimentation in design (McHarg) 44

explicit knowledge 14

exploration 16–17, 19, 67, 130–1

exploratory drawing 8, 134, 154

extensions 96–100, 102–3

extension transference (ET) 100–2, 103

externalized approaches 101

fertility 12

field sketching 6, 9, 62–5; Alhambra (Granada, Spain) *64*; *Cloud Gate* sculpture *89*; collage-style drawing *73*; forms and geometries *67*; landscape and greenhouse structure *63*; museum-housed carriages *75*; and practice design 74; public park and Petronas Twin Towers *61*; vernacular floating village *69*; vertical forms in temple complex *70*; Yu Garden (Old City, Shanghai) *66*

flow *141*

fluidly 8, 36

form ever follows function (Sullivan) 35–8, 44–5

form-finding: exercises 48–58; experiments *136*

form must follow more than just function (McHarg) 33

forms 36, 41–2, 46–8

fortress wall and gate (Avignon, France) *4*

frame-to-frame exercises 49

freefall law (Galileo) 71–2

function 41–2

Galileo Galilei 66, 71–3

garden and pool (Alhambra, Granada, Spain) *7*

gardens 39–40

Gaudí, Antoni *1*

geometry 65–7, 74

gesture images *149*

give-and-take presentations 99

good design 2–3, 44, 118, 124, 153

Grand Palace, Bangkok (Thailand) *70*

Grand Turk Island (Turks and Caicos Islands) *73*

green sea turtles sketch *36*

habitual techniques 125

Hall, Edward T. 97, 99, 100–1, 103

hand-drawn experimental images 48

Henri, Robert 120, 121–3, 125

herons 149–50

horses galloping sketches *100*

Hunt, William Morris 124–5

INDEX 161

idea-in-mind 120
ideas 117, 134
imagination 137–8
implicit knowledge 14–15
improvisation 135
individuality (uniqueness) 87
ingenuity 12
initiation (observational learning) 93
inner precedents 105–7
innovation 6, 13, 124–5
intercessions 46, 47
interpretation 130–1
interpretive center imagining *93*
intersecting volumes *12*
inventiveness 12–13

Jardin du Luxembourg (Paris,
    France) *2*

knowledge 14–16

Lake Tahoe (Nevada) *83*
landscape architectural design 44, 47
landscape architecture 1–6, 157
landscapes: aesthetics 40;
    intercessions 46; and intersecting
    volumes *12*
learning 96
left-brain and right-brain theories
    (L+R) 13–14
light pencil lines 21
"living machine" at shoreline image
    15
low-impact and low-touch structural
    forms *155*

Malham Cove (Yorkshire Dales, UK)
    118
mathematics 67–74
McHarg, Ian 38–45
Mekong River (Cambodia) *69*
memory (observational learning) 92

methods and media 20–4
migration exercises 30–1
Millennium Park (Chicago) *89*
mimicry 125
motivation (observational learning)
    93
motorcycle sketches *83*
motor (observational learning) 93
movement and interpretation 130–1
move, merge and mingle exercises
    28–9
multiple interpretations 75

native calligraphic form *102*
native plant forms design exploration
    117
natural ecologies 44
natural features 112–13
naturalized gardens 41
natural systems 38, 39, 42, 124
    see also ecology
nature area 140–3
nature–human interventions 42
nature-teacher design model 41
negative space corridors *17*
neighborhood pocket park 144–7
neurological research 14, 62
Newton, N. T. 3
Noether, Emmy 68–9
non-photo blue pencils 21

observational learning 91–6
observation-based design
    experiments 91–2
observation–conversation
    interchange 95
observations 87–91
on-site sketching 74–5
ordering systems *79*
originality 12, 87
original techniques 125
orthogonal pavement *118*

162   INDEX

Parc Güell, Barcelona (Gaudí) *1*
Paris (France) 2, 7
passages design exploration *129*
pavilion 148, 150–2
personal adventures 155–7
Petronas Twin Towers (Kuala
     Lumpur, Malaysia) *61*
physical attributes 120, 126
place-making 119–20
practicing design 74, 88
Preah Khan Temple (Angkor,
     Cambodia) *137*
precedents 105–7
pre-engineered solutions 103
pre-packaged sources 118
problem-solving 3

radially segmented landform *134*
rails-to-trails greenway walking and
     bicycle system 144
regional-scale notions 42
resisting transference 103
resourcefulness 12
rest-stop park space 144–5
retention (observational learning)
     92
rhizomes design exploration *154*
rigging of design 118
roots design exploration *154*
round robin exercises 26–7
ruin-like space sketch *137*
Ryerson, Margery 121

Schönbrunn Palace (Vienna, Austria)
     75
second-tier observations 74–5
self-generated precedents 105–7
self-learning 87–8
semi-arid landscapes *83*
sequential view-framing *66*
side-by-side drawings 76–7
site language 94

sites: meaning 90–1; as models 94
sketchbooks 20
sketching 60–2
social ecologies 44
Socrates 130
space-efficient town *95*
spatial geometries 6
spiral growth development *37*
stampeding oxen sketch *123*
"state-of-the-art" 103
stimulating individuals 122
study of form *24*
Sullivan, Louis 35–8, 44–5
surfacing techniques *127*
systems (McHarg) 38

tangible expressions 117
teacher–student mode 96
technique 120
templates 6, 103
temple complex (Grand Palace,
     Bangkok) *70*
terraced landscapes *104*
"the trap" (Hall) 103
three-frame sequences 51–4, 55–7
three-step translations *83*
tools (Hall) 97
Tour Eiffel (Paris, France) *7*
transit-oriented development (TOD)
     106
translations 77–83
two-step translations 74, *82*, *83*

uniqueness (individuality) 87
urgency 3

Valley of the Kings (Luxor, Egypt)
     82
values 38
vernacular floating village *69*
village sketch *40*
visual alertness 154

visual discussions, experimental drawings 97–8

Vitruvius 4, 153

wading birds habitat restoration 149–50

water-harvesting pavilion form *73*

weathered landforms *156*

wetland nature preserve *98*, 148–52

wildlife habitat design exploration *90*

wonder 126, 130

wood-grain patterns *125*

word-gaming exercises 110–13

Yu Garden (Old City, Shanghai, China) *66*